2

AVENUES
English Grammar

Lynne Gaetz

TEACHER'S ANNOTATED **EDITION**

Montréal

Managing Editor
Sharnee Chait

Editor
Lucie Turcotte

Copy Editor
Stacey Berman

Proofreader
Katie Moore

Coordinator, Rights and Permissions
Pierre Richard Bernier

Photo Research and Permissions
Marie-Chantal Masson

Art Director
Hélène Cousineau

Graphic Design Coordinator
Lyse LeBlanc

Book Design and Layout
Interscript

Cover Design
Frédérique Bouvier

Cover Artwork
Pietro Adamo. *Citta Series*, 2009. Mixed media on canvas,
40 x 40 inches. Courtesy of Progressive Fine Art and Galerie
Beauchamp. © 2011 Artist Pietro Adamo.

© ÉDITIONS DU RENOUVEAU PÉDAGOGIQUE INC. (ERPI), 2012
ERPI publishes and distributes PEARSON ELT products in Canada.

5757 Cypihot Street
Saint-Laurent, Québec H4S 1R3
CANADA
Telephone: 1 800 263-3678
Fax: 1 866 334-0448
infoesl@pearsonerpi.com
http://pearsonelt.ca

Registration of copyright – Bibliothèque et Archives nationales du Québec, 2012
Registration of copyright – Library and Archives Canada, 2012

Printed in Canada   123456789   II 16 15 14 13 12
ISBN 978-2-7613-4582-8   134582 ABCD   ENV94

Acknowledgements
Many people helped produce what you hold in your hands.
I would like to express sincere thanks to

- Sharnee Chait for her valuable expertise;
- Lucie Turcotte for her patience and insight while
  editing this book;
- Julie Hough for her enthusiasm which helped ignite
  this project;
- My students at Collège Lionel-Groulx for their
  insightful feedback;
- Diego Pelaez for his valuable contributions to
  this manuscript and the Companion Website;
- Interscript for the creative layout.

Finally, I dedicate this to my husband Octavio and
to my children Diego and Rebeka.

This book is printed on paper made in Québec from 100% post-consumer
recycled materials, processed chlorine-free, certified Eco-Logo, and
manufactured using biogas energy.

TABLE OF CONTENTS

UNIT 1

Nouns and Determiners

You can present the grammar units in any order that you prefer. This unit contains information about various topics and can be used with any skills chapter.

Preview

WHAT IS A NOUN?

A **noun** is a person, place, or thing. A **count noun** can be counted and has a plural form. A **noncount noun** cannot be counted and has only a singular form. Often, noncount nouns refer to categories of objects or abstract concepts.

noncount noun
We had a lot of **homework**.

count noun
We have three **assignments**.

TRAVEL SUPPLIES

PART A

Work with a partner or a team of students. Imagine that you are about to go backpacking to another country for two weeks. List the items that you will need for your trip. Use your dictionary if necessary.

Clothing and Sleeping Supplies	Medical Supplies	Personal Items and Documents
(Possible answers)	(Possible answers)	(Possible answers)
backpack, tent, sleeping bag	adhesive bandages	driver's licence
pillow and blanket	scissors	passport
sandals or running shoes	cotton ear swabs	shampoo and soap
socks and underwear	cotton balls	brush and comb
T-shirts and sweaters	peroxide	flashlight and sewing kit
pants and shorts	antibiotic cream	portable cooking stove
hat, gloves, and scarf	painkillers	pots, pans, and cutlery
bathing suit	bug spray	matches

PART B

Now imagine that you are on a deserted island. You can only have five of the items that you listed above. Discuss which five items are the most important and explain why.

_____   _____   _____

_____   _____   _____

Nouns and Determiners: Forms and Usage

NOUNS

Nouns are words that refer to people, places, or things. Most nouns have singular and plural forms.

SPELLING OF REGULAR PLURAL FORMS

	SINGULAR	PLURAL
Most plural nouns simply end in –s.	student house	students houses
Add –es to nouns ending in –s, –ch, –sh, –x, or –z.	kiss match	kisses matches
Add –s or –es to nouns ending in –o.	piano potato	pianos potatoes
When nouns end in –f or –fe, change the –f or –fe to –v and add –es.	shelf knife	shelves knives
When nouns end in a consonant + –y, change –y to –ies. When nouns end in a vowel + –y, just add –s.	lottery day	lotteries days

SPELLING OF IRREGULAR PLURAL FORMS

Some nouns have irregular plural forms. These irregular forms do not need an additional –s.

child ▶ children	goose ▶ geese	person ▶ people
fish ▶ fish	man ▶ men	tooth ▶ teeth
foot ▶ feet	mouse ▶ mice	woman ▶ women

Most style guides treat *media* as a plural noun. However, many newspapers, magazines, and websites treat *media* as a singular collective noun when it refers to the Internet, television, newspapers, film, and radio. Decide which usage you prefer.

Some nouns are borrowed from foreign languages and keep the plural form of the original language.

analysis ▶ analyses	paparazzo ▶ paparazzi
bacterium ▶ bacteria	phenomenon ▶ phenomena

PLURAL NOUNS WITH A SINGULAR MEANING

Some nouns always have a plural form but a singular meaning.

economics	mathematics	mechanics
news	politics	physics

My brother studied **physics**. Now he is taking a course in **mechanics**.

PLURAL NOUNS WITH A PLURAL MEANING

Some nouns appear only in the plural form. The object or idea might have two or more parts but is considered a singular entity. Use a plural verb with these nouns.

binoculars	credentials	goods	scissors
clothes	glasses	savings	shorts

My **clothes** are dirty. Your **glasses** are in your pocket.

COUNT AND NONCOUNT NOUNS

Count nouns refer to people, places, or things that you can count, such as *girl* or *toy*. Count nouns have both a singular and a plural form.

We own a **car**. My brother has two **cars**.

Noncount nouns cannot be counted. They have only a singular form.

We have too much **homework**. We need more **equipment**.

To express the quantity of a noncount noun, we use expressions that describe amounts, such as *types of*, *a lot of*, or *pieces of*. Note that the noncount noun remains singular.

We need <u>a lot of</u> **information**. We ate four <u>slices of</u> **bread**.

COMMON NONCOUNT NOUNS

CATEGORIES OF OBJECTS		FOOD	NATURE AND SUBSTANCES	ABSTRACT NOUNS	
baggage	machinery	bread	air	advice	knowledge
clothing	mail	cheese	chalk	attention	luck
equipment	makeup	fish	coal	behaviour	peace
furniture	money	honey	electricity	education	progress
homework	music	meat	fur	effort	proof
housework	postage	milk	hair	evidence	research
ink	software	rice	paint	health	time**
jewellery	wildlife	salt	radiation	help	trouble
luggage	work*	sugar	weather	information	violence

* *Work* is a noncount noun except when you refer to artistic works.

** *Time* is a noncount noun when you refer to *free time* or *spare time*.

DETERMINERS

DETERMINERS WITH COUNT AND NONCOUNT NOUNS

COUNT NOUNS	NONCOUNT NOUNS	COUNT AND NONCOUNT NOUNS
Many **Few / A Few**	**Much** **Little / A Little**	**A Lot Of** **Some**
Paris has **many** museums. Very **few** people are there. **A few** museums are closed.	I have too **much** work. I have very **little** time. Do you have **a little** money?	I took **a lot of** photos. Do you have **some** time?

USING *THIS*, *THAT*, *THESE*, AND *THOSE*

TERM	USAGE	EXAMPLE
this (singular) **these** (plural)	refers to things that are near the speaker in time or place	**This** burger is good. **These** fries are also tasty. **These** days, it is sunny.
that (singular) **those** (plural)	refers to things that are far from the speaker in time or place	Do you see **those** people in **that** store? In 2011, there were severe floods, so **that** was a difficult year.

ARTICLES

TERM	USAGE	EXAMPLE
a, an	refers to a general person, place, or thing	Karim needs **a** new car. He wants **an** Audi.
the	refers to one or more specific nouns	**The** cars in that showroom are expensive.

For extra practice with nouns and determiners, visit the Companion Website.

Practice

EXERCISE 1 IDENTIFY PLURAL ERRORS

Correct fifteen errors in the underlined plural nouns. Write *C* above the plural nouns that are correct.

 companies
EXAMPLE: Many <u>companys</u> break the law.

1. I often watch the <u>news</u> on television. I am interested
    politics   countries   people   lives
    in <u>politic</u>. In many <u>countrys</u>, <u>persons</u> have difficult <u>lifes</u>.

2. In Vietnam and China, the <u>salarys</u> are very low. For example,
                                    salaries
                                women   hours
    in the shoe industry, some <u>womens</u> work for many <u>hour</u>.
                C   ladies   men
    For seven <u>days</u> a week, many <u>ladys</u> and <u>mans</u> stand
                                                          feet
    in assembly lines. They stand on their <u>feets</u> a lot.

3. In some <u>places</u>, <u>familys</u> ask their <u>childs</u> to work in <u>factorys</u>.
            C   families   children   factories
                                            knives
    Small girls and boys use sharp <u>knifes</u> and other dangerous
        C
    <u>objects</u>.

4. People who study <u>economic</u> should learn about child labour.
                        economics

SPECIAL RULES

Singular

Use a singular noun after *each* and *every*.

<u>Each</u> **day**, Max cleans <u>every</u> **room** in his house.

Adjectives are always singular. (An adjective describes a noun or pronoun.)

    other   **great**

I have ~~others~~ priorities.   These are ~~greats~~ deals.

Be careful—sometimes nouns act as adjectives.

I have eight **dollars**.   BUT   She has a twenty-**dollar** <u>coat</u>.
Dollar is a noun and takes an s.   *Dollar is acting as an adjective to describe coat.*

Plural

Use a plural noun after the expression *one of the*.

<u>One of the</u> most difficult **jobs** is nursing.

EXERCISE 2 SINGULAR AND PLURAL NOUNS

Underline the appropriate nouns or adjectives below.

EXAMPLE: Some (student / <u>students</u>) live in the suburbs.

1. Each English-speaking (<u>nation</u> / nations) has unique characteristics. In England, most (person / persons / <u>people</u>) are aware of social class. One of the most obvious (difference / <u>differences</u>) between classes is the accent. An upper class (<u>citizen</u> / citizens) has a "posh" accent.

2. In Ireland, most (man / mans / <u>men</u>) and (woman / womans / <u>women</u>) are friendly. In pubs, the patrons chat and sing (<u>beautiful</u> / beautifuls) (song / <u>songs</u>) together. Sometimes, (familys / family / <u>families</u>) bring their (childs / <u>children</u> / childrens) to the pub. Samuel, a seventeen-(<u>year</u> / years)-old student from Dublin, can stay in pubs until 9 pm. However, customers must be eighteen (year / <u>years</u>) old to be served alcohol.

3. New Zealand has (<u>several</u> / severals) (<u>specific</u> / specifics) (feature / <u>features</u>). Most people live on two (<u>main</u> / mains) (island / <u>islands</u>). Every (<u>man</u> / mans / men) and (<u>woman</u> / womans / women) who lives there is called a "Kiwi." The name derives from the flightless bird, not from the green fruit. One of my best (friend / <u>friends</u>) is a kiwi.

EXERCISE 3 WRITE COUNT AND NONCOUNT NOUNS

You can ask students to do Exercise 3 with a partner. Make it a timed competition. Forbid students from looking in the answer key until the competition is over.

Describe what you see in the pictures. First, decide what the category is. (The category is a noncount noun.) Then, list the items. Write *a*, *an*, or a number before each item.

Category: furniture

Items: a sofa

a bar and three stools

a TV stand

a carpet

two coffee tables

a lamp

an end table

Category: money

Items: a penny

a twenty-dollar bill

a loonie

two quarters

a toonie

a five-dollar bill

Category: makeup

Items: a compact

lipstick

a makeup brush

mascara

nail polish

an eyebrow pencil

EXERCISE 4 IDENTIFY PLURAL NOUNS

Change the italicized words to the plural form (if necessary). If you can't use the plural form, write *X* in the spaces provided. Be careful, because some words are noncount nouns. For a list of common noncount nouns, see page 3.

EXAMPLE: I have two *watch*_es_ . She needs more *information* _X_ .

1. I did some *research*_X_ on the history of Canadian shopping malls. Before 1950, there were no shopping *mall*_s_ in Canada. Shoppers went to individual _X_ *store*_s_ to buy their *food*_X_, *clothing*_X_, and *furniture*_X_. Then, when *suburb*_s_ grew, malls followed.

2. In September 1950, developers built the first open-*air*_X_ mall in Vancouver. Three _X_ *year*_s_ later, Henry Morgan opened a mall in Montreal. At the time, it was one of the largest shopping *centre*_s_ in North America. During the next thirty *year*_s_, almost every *town*_X_ and *city*_X_ in Canada built a shopping *centre*_X_.

3. Soon, *developer*_s_ across Canada competed to build larger and larger *shopping*_X_ *mall*_s_. In 1981, the Ghermezian *brother*_s_ spent a lot of *money*_X_ to build the gigantic West Edmonton Mall. The mall has more than eight-*hundred*_X_ *store*_s_ and *service*_s_. It also includes a water *park*_X_ and a *hotel*_X_. During a twenty-three-*year*_X_ period, until 2004, it was the largest mall in the world.

EXERCISE 5 IDENTIFY ERRORS

Identify and correct six errors with noncount nouns.

                                                traffic
EXAMPLE: When I drive to work, there is a lot of traffics.

1.   research
   Dr. Chris Chu does a lot of researches about suntanning.
               evidence
   There is a lot of evidences that tanning booths are dangerous for the health. These booths can cause many different types of skin cancer. Dr. Chu has a lot of
              knowledge
   knowledges about melanoma, the deadliest form of skin cancer.

2.   time   information
   During his free times, Chu looks for informations about
             advice
   melanoma. Chu gives this advices to his patients: Use a spray tan instead of a tanning booth.

MANY, MUCH, FEW, AND LITTLE

Use **many** with count nouns in affirmative, negative, and question forms. Use **much** with noncount nouns. Only use *much* in negative and question forms. In affirmative forms, use *a lot* instead of *much*, unless you refer to an excessive amount of something, such as *too much* or *so much*.

How **much** <u>money</u> do you have? Eric doesn't have **much** <u>work</u>.
He has too **much** <u>free time</u> these days.

Use **few** with count nouns and **little** with noncount nouns. Note that there are slight differences in meaning when you use "a" before *few* and *little*.

Few and **little** mean "almost none."

A few and **a little** mean "a small amount."

She has very **few** friends.

She has **little** free time.
(These are complaints.)

She has **a few** friends.

She has **a little** free time.
(She is okay with the situation.)

TIP

Money

When you enquire about a price, ask "***How much is it***?" The word *money* is implied.

How much (money) is the train ticket?

EXERCISE 6 *MUCH, MANY, FEW,* AND *LITTLE*

PART A

Write *much* or *many* in each space below.

EXAMPLE: I have <u>many</u> ideas about the project.

1. _____Many_____ people travel around the world to visit famous sites. One of Montreal's most distinctive landmarks is Habitat 67. People did not have _____much_____ knowledge about design, and _____many_____ citizens complained about the style of the building. At first, there were _____many_____ critics. With its gray blocks, Habitat 67 looks like a cubist sculpture. How _____much_____ did the building cost? It cost about $22 million. For _____many_____ years, Montrealers did not appreciate their architectural marvel. They did not pay _____much_____ attention to it.

PART B

Write *little* or *few* in each space below.

EXAMPLE: Safdie did a <u>little</u> research.

2. In 1964, Montreal was preparing for the EXPO 67 celebrations. A _____few_____ architects competed to design an apartment complex in Old Montreal. They received very _____little_____ information in advance. The city wanted the building to have a _____few_____ unique features. At that time, Moshe Safdie had very _____little_____ time to prepare for the competition. His McGill master's thesis was about a housing complex that looked like children's toy building blocks. His design won. Safdie had very _____few_____ problems with his design. A _____few_____ years later, Habitat 67 opened.

THIS, THAT, THESE, AND THOSE

This and **these** refer to people and things that are physically close to the speaker in time or place.

Near the speaker
This (singular)
These (plural)

That and **those** refer to people and things that are physically distant from the speaker in time or place.

Far from the speaker
That (singular)
Those (plural)

Singular	**This** is my bike. **This** year, I will buy a car.	**That** is my sister's car. I liked 2005; **that** was a great year.
Plural	**These** glasses are mine. I feel tired **these** days.	**Those** cars are going too fast. Remember the 1990s? **Those** years were great.

EXERCISE 7 IDENTIFY ERRORS

Correct ten errors in the underlined words below. If the word is correct, write *C* above it.

EXAMPLE: <u>This</u> shoes are tight. I really like <u>those</u> shoes that you are wearing.
(These) (C)

1. Angela was born in 1978 and grew up during the 1980s. <u>These</u> were difficult (Those)

    years because her family did not have <u>much</u> money. Angela showed me a (C)

    photograph from <u>this</u> time. In the photo, her parents look very tired. (that)

2. Today, Angela is happy. <u>This</u> days, she is doing really well. She has a good job as (These)

    a journalist. Right now, Angela and I are reading <u>this</u> newspapers that are on the (these)

    table. They are interesting. There are <u>much</u> good articles. (many)

3. Look outside! Across the street, there are so <u>much</u> people. Why are <u>that</u> people (many) (those)

    running? Why is <u>this</u> police car driving so fast? Perhaps <u>those</u> workers are (that) (C)

    protesting. They have <u>much</u> complaints. Wow, now <u>many</u> reporters are (many) (C)

    watching the action. They are taking <u>much</u> photos of the crowd. (many)

POSSESSIVE FORM OF NOUNS

Singular Nouns

Add *apostrophe –s ('s)* to singular nouns to indicate possession.

That is the child of Anne. That is **Anne's** child.

If the noun ends in –s, you must still add *apostrophe –s*.

That car belongs to Ross. That is **Ross's** car.

Plural Nouns

When a plural noun ends in –s, add an apostrophe to indicate ownership.

The **boys'** bedrooms are in the basement.

Add *apostrophe –s ('s)* to irregular plural nouns.

The **men's** room is down the hall.

EXERCISE 8 POSSESSIVE NOUNS

Write the possessive forms of the following phrases.

EXAMPLE: the sister of Josh — Josh's sister

1. the coat of the child — the child's coat
2. the shoes of the children — the children's shoes
3. the desk of the employee — the employee's desk
4. the entrance of the employees — the employees' entrance
5. the book of the student — the student's book
6. the pottery of the students — the students' pottery
7. the house of Mr. Green — Mr. Green's house
8. the car of the Greens — the Greens' car
9. the restroom of the men — the men's restroom

A, AN, AND THE

A and *an* are general articles. They mean "one." Place *a* or *an* before a singular noun.

Use **a** before words that begin with a consonant: **a** friend, **a** house.

Exception: When *u* sounds like "you," put *a* before it: **a** union, **a** university

Use **an** before words that begin with a vowel: **an** apple, **an** umbrella.

Exception: Use *an* before words that begin with a silent *h:* **an** hour, **an** honest man.

Use **the** to indicate a specific noun (or specific nouns). *The* can be placed before both singular and plural nouns.

general   specific

I need to find **a** new suitcase. **The** luggage in that store is expensive.

TIP

The

Do not put *the* before the following:

▪ sports	▶ He plays soccer.
▪ languages	▶ She speaks Mandarin.
▪ most city, province, state, or country names (Some exceptions are the United States and the Netherlands.)	▶ Roma lives in Israel. Isaac is moving to France.
▪ meals	▶ I will eat breakfast.

EXERCISE 9 *A, AN,* OR *THE*

Write *a*, *an*, *the*, or *X* (for "nothing") in the spaces provided.

EXAMPLE: I took ____a____ university course that was very interesting.

1. I read ____a____ famous novel called *Lost Horizon* by James Hilton. Hilton is not from ____X____ Mexico, ____X____ Canada, or ____the____ United States. He is from ____X____ England. His novel is about ____a____ utopian world.

2. At the beginning of ____the____ novel, three classmates are in ____X____ London during ____the____ spring. They are eating ____X____ lunch and remembering their friend, Hugh Conway. Conway is ____a____ British diplomat who speaks ____X____ English and ____X____ French. He is also ____an____ athlete who excels in ____X____ soccer. He is ____an____ honest man. He mysteriously disappears during ____an____ airplane flight to ____X____ Asia.

3. The plane lands on ____a____ Himalayan mountaintop. The crash kills ____the____ pilot and destroys ____the____ plane. ____The____ four survivors arrive in ____a____ strange town. They spend a few days in ____a____ hospital, and then they go to ____a____ hotel. They stay during ____the____ summer and ____the____ fall.

4. ____The____ town, called Shangri-La, has ____an____ unusual characteristic: The town's citizens have ____X____ very long lives. For example, ____the____ leader of the monastery is more than 300 years old. Conway compares the peacefulness in ____the____ town to ____the____ violence in the rest of ____the____ world. Conway decides that he wants to live to ____an____ old age in Shangri-La.

Another and A Lot

Another is written as one word. **A lot** is always written as two words.

      another   **a lot**

I want ~~an other~~ MP3 player. Marcus Mumford has written ~~alot~~ of songs.

All Day and Every Day

All day means "during a complete day." Do not put *the* before *all*, and do not make *day* plural.

Every day means "regularly on more than one day."

                           all day

Yesterday, I spoke English ~~all days~~ with my friend. I try to practise every day.

EXERCISE 10 NOUNS, ARTICLES, AND DETERMINERS

Underline the correct answer in parentheses.

1. Ten years ago, in my psychology class, I studied laughter. (This / These / <u>Those</u>) classes began just after (the / <u>X</u>) breakfast. During each (<u>class</u> / classes), we talked about laughter theories. Sometimes, my friends and I would laugh all (the / <u>X</u>) day. We had (<u>a lot</u> / alot) of fun. It was one of the best (course / <u>courses</u>) that I have ever taken.

2. While doing my (<u>homework</u> / homeworks), I learned that almost everyone can laugh. Even a two-(<u>month</u> / months)-old child is able to laugh. Some (person / <u>people</u> / persons) laugh more than others, and some can't laugh. For example, in 1909, there was a thirty-two-(<u>year</u> / years)-old woman who could not laugh out loud. It is (<u>a</u> / an / X) very rare condition.

3. (Man / <u>Men</u> / Mans) and (woman / <u>women</u> / womans) have different ideas about humour. In a study, (man's / mens / <u>men's</u>) and (womans / <u>women's</u> / womens) brainwaves were examined while they were watching a comedy. They laughed at (<u>different</u> / differents) things.

4. (An other / <u>Another</u>) study looked at (persons / peoples / <u>people's</u>) preferences in mates. Most females wanted (a / <u>an</u>) amicable partner who would make them laugh. (Much / <u>Many</u>) males wanted a partner who would laugh at their jokes.

5. Last month, it rained (all day / <u>every day</u>) for a few hours. I spent too (much / <u>many</u>) hours indoors. Today, it also looks like it will rain (all days / all the day / <u>all day</u>). Still, I will try to appreciate each (<u>moment</u> / moments).

Answer the following questions. If you don't know an answer, go back and review the appropriate section.

1. Do noncount nouns have plural forms?　　Yes　No

2. Write *much* or *many* before each word.

   a) ___many___ people   c) ___many___ men   e) ___much___ equipment

   b) ___much___ information   d) ___many___ children   f) ___many___ students

3. What is the difference between *few* and *little*?

   ___Use *few* before count nouns and *little* before noncount nouns.___

4. Correct the errors in the following sentences.

   　　　　　　　　　　a lot　　　　　　　　　　　　　　year
   a) My friend travels to ~~alot~~ of different places every ~~years~~.

   　　　　　　　　　　　cities　　　　　　　　　　　　　little
   b) One of his favourite ~~city~~ is Shanghai, but I have very ~~few~~

      information
      ~~informations~~ about that city.

   　　　　　　　　　　　other　people
   c) He never travels with ~~others~~ ~~peoples~~.

   　　　　　　　　　　　the　　　　　　　　　　the
   d) Last month, he was in ~~the~~ Brazil, and he played ~~the~~ soccer
      with some Brazilians.

   　　　　　　　　　　　Those
   e) Look out the window. ~~That~~ cars are driving really fast.

Need more practice?
Visit the Companion Website and try additional exercises.

Final Review

You can use the Final Review as a test. There are twenty-five answers. You can also find additional practice exercises and testing material on the Companion Website.

Underline the correct word in parentheses. Note that *X* means "nothing."

EXAMPLE: I am very busy (these / those) days.

1. Neil Pasricha does not live in (the / X) United States. He lives near (a / the / X) Toronto, and his father and mother are from (the / X) Nairobi and (the / X) India. Neil is not athletic, although he likes (the / X / a) baseball.

2. In early 2008, Neil Pasricha felt bored. Also at (this / that) time, his best friend was very depressed. (These / Those) months were difficult. In June 2008,

Pasricha decided to create a blog about happiness. He worked on his blog (all days / each day). In his blog, he wanted to remind his friend and (other / others) (persons / people / peoples) about the (special / specials) joys in life.

3. His blog describes (much / many) great moments, such as wearing underwear straight out of the dryer or taking the first scoop of peanut butter from the jar. At first, Pasricha made very (few / little) money from his blog. However, a (little / few) months later, the blog became really popular.

4. In 2009, the thirty-one-(years / year)-old man still had (a lot / alot) of (personals / personal) problems. Pasricha's wife of one year decided she didn't love him anymore, and she left him. However, Pasricha spent very (few / little) time in despair. Pasricha says he cried for several (week / weeks / week's), but then he found some (information / informations) about the positive effects of crying on the body.

5. How (much / many) attention did the blog receive? In 2009, Pasricha's blog received more than ten (million / millions) visitors. Clearly, he attracted (peoples / peoples' / people's) attention. Soon, a publisher contacted him. In 2010, the publisher turned Pasricha's blog into a book. His fifteen-(dollar / dollars) book was one of the most successful (book / book's / books) of the year.

SPEAKING AND WRITING

Students do the writing exercise on a separate sheet of paper. Once students have finished, ask them to exchange their writing and peer edit for the correct use of verbs.

Recall Game

Your class will be divided into four teams. Each team will receive a box filled with everyday household items such as school supplies, personal maintenance items, health supplies, and tools. You and your team will have one minute to look at the items in your box and memorize them. Then you must try to recall what your box contains. Make a list of the singular and plural items in your box. Then write a paragraph, and use the names of some of the items in your paragraph.

Present Tenses

Preview

WHAT ARE PRESENT TENSES?

The **simple present** indicates general truths, facts, habitual actions, and customs.

The **present progressive** describes temporary situations, or actions that are in progress.

fact
I **have** several courses.

in progress
Right now, I **am reading** this book.

FIND THE DIFFERENCES

Look at the following two photos.

A.

B.

What is different in Photo B? On a separate sheet of paper, write complete sentences about six differences.

EXAMPLE: In B, there is a red building in the distance.

Present Tenses: Forms and Usage

Compare the **simple present** and the **present progressive** tenses.

Nadia **drives** to Halifax every month.
(simple present)

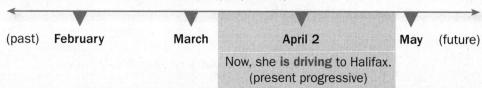

| (past) | **February** | **March** | **April 2** | **May** | (future) |

Now, she **is driving** to Halifax.
(present progressive)

	SIMPLE PRESENT (GENERAL)	**PRESENT PROGRESSIVE (NOW)**
FORM	I You We They } work. He She It } works.	I am + talk + –ing. He, She, It is + talk + –ing. You, We, They are + talk + –ing.
USAGE	The **simple present** indicates general truths, facts, habitual actions, and customs. Montreal **has** a subway system. (fact) Dominique **skis** every winter. (habit) Devout Muslims **fast** during Ramadan. (custom) **Keywords**: always, often, usually, sometimes, seldom, rarely, never, every day ...	The **present progressive** indicates that an action is happening now, or for a present, temporary period of time. Currently, we **are reading** this book. (now) This week, Ann **is visiting** us. (temporary period of time) **Keywords**: now, at this moment, currently, today, these days, this week, this month, this morning, nowadays ...
QUESTION	Put *do* or *does* before the subject. Use the base form of the verb. **Do** you travel often? **Does** she have a passport? **Exception**: *be* **Is** Julie late? **Are** you busy?	Put *be* before the subject. **Am** I bothering you? **Is** she sleeping now? **Are** they staying with us?
NEGATIVE	Add *do* or *does* with *not*. Julie **does not** complain. (doesn't) They **do not** own a car. (don't) **Exception**: *be* They **are not** late. (aren't)	Add *not*. He is **not** sleeping right now. (isn't) They are **not** working today. (aren't)

SIMPLE PRESENT: SPELLING RULES

RULE	EXAMPLE	THIRD-PERSON SINGULAR FORM
Add –s to the end of most verbs. **Exception:** *have* becomes *has*.	talk read	talk**s** read**s**
When verbs end in –s, –sh, –ss, –ch, –o, or –x, add –es.	wish go	wish**es** go**es**
When verbs end in a consonant + –y, change to –ies. When verbs end in a vowel + –y, keep the –y and add –s.	marry study stay	marr**ies** stud**ies** stay**s**

PRESENT PROGRESSIVE: SPELLING RULES

RULE	EXAMPLE	–*ING* FORM
When verbs end in silent –e, delete the –e and add –*ing*.	write	writ**ing**
When verbs end in –y, just add –*ing*.	try, play	try**ing**, play**ing**
When verbs end in –ie, change –ie to –y and add –*ing*.	lie	l**ying**
When verbs end in consonant-vowel-consonant, double the last letter and add –*ing*. **Exception:** words that end in –x or –w (snow ▶ snowing)	stop jog	stop**ping** jog**ging**
When multi-syllabic verbs end in a **stressed** consonant-vowel-consonant, double the last letter and add –*ing*.	re**fer** be**gin**	refer**ring** begin**ning**
But if the last syllable is not stressed, just add –*ing*.	**o**pen **hap**pen	open**ing** happen**ing**

PRONUNCIATION HELP WITH ONLINE DICTIONARIES

Many dictionaries are available online. On some sites, such as *dictionary.reference. com*, the stressed syllable is indicated in bold, and by clicking on the loudspeaker icon, you can hear the pronunciation of the word.

be · gin · ning   ◀)) [bih-**gin**-ing]

NON-PROGRESSIVE VERBS

Some verbs are rarely used in the progressive tense.

    loves   **wants**
Kara ~~is loving~~ hockey. She ~~is wanting~~ to compete.

PERCEPTION		PREFERENCE		MENTAL STATE/OPINION		POSSESSION
appear	smell*	appreciate	like	believe	recognize	belong
feel*	sound	care	love	doubt	remember	have*
hear	resemble	desire	need	forget	think*	own
see	taste*	envy	prefer	know	trust	possess
seem		hate	want	mean	understand	
				realize		

* Some verbs have more than one meaning and can be used in the progressive tense.
  Compare the following:
  I **think** it is expensive. (Expresses an opinion) / I **am thinking** about it.
  He **has** many clothes. (Expresses ownership) / He **is having** a bad day.

THERE + BE

There is means that something exists. *There* is a false subject, and the real subject follows the verb *be*.

There is: one person or thing

There are: two or more people or things

There is a suitcase by the door.

There are many people at the airport.

Question form: In questions, move the verb *be* before *there*.

Is there a bus? **Are** there many taxis?

Practice

EXERCISE 1 *THERE IS* OR *THERE ARE*

PART A

List the items in the suitcase. Use *There is* or *There are*. Also use the expression *a pair of*.

EXAMPLE: There is a computer.

1. There are three books.
2. There is a pair of socks.
3. There are three pairs of pants.
4. There is a hair brush.
5. There are two shirts.
6. There are two ties.
7. There is a camera.
8. There is a computer.

PART B

Write four questions about the photo in Part A.

EXAMPLE: Is there a computer?

9. Answers will vary.
10. _____
11. _____
12. _____

SPECIAL SUBJECTS

Indefinite pronouns beginning with *every–*, *some–*, *any–*, and *no–* are considered singular. To help you remember this rule, note that the last part of each word (*body*, *thing*, etc.) is singular.

everybody	everyone	everything	everywhere
somebody	someone	something	somewhere
nobody	no one	nothing	nowhere

Everybody **wants** some coffee, but nobody **has** any money.

Sometimes a **gerund** (*–ing* form of the verb) is the subject of a sentence. The subject is considered third-person singular, so you must add *–s* or *–es* to the verb.

Fishing **requires** specific equipment.

TIP

Interrupting Words

Words that come between the subject and verb may confuse you. In these cases, identify the subject and make sure that the verb agrees with the subject.

The <u>ticket</u> that I bought online **has** several restrictions.

EXERCISE 2 SUBJECT-VERB AGREEMENT

Underline the correct present tense verbs.

EXAMPLE: Prague (<u>is</u> / are) one of the most popular tourist destinations in Europe.

1. What (<u>is</u> / are) the best city in the world? Every year, *The Economist* (conduct / <u>conducts</u>) a survey. People from many different countries (<u>answer</u> / answers) questions about their city's safety, education, health care, and environment. Large multinational companies (<u>use</u> / uses) the data to decide where to open offices or factories.

2. The city of Geneva, in Switzerland, usually (get / <u>gets</u>) a high score in the survey. But this year, Vancouver is the number one city. Almost everybody (like / <u>likes</u>) Vancouver. The city, which (<u>has</u> / have) an amazing location, (<u>is</u> / are) near the ocean and the Rocky Mountains. Nobody (worry / <u>worries</u>) about winter in Vancouver because the city (have / <u>has</u>) very little snow. Rain, however, (<u>is</u> / are) common on the West Coast. Everybody (spend / <u>spends</u>) time outdoors. Almost nobody (stay / <u>stays</u>) inside when the weather is nice.

Vancouver Harbour

3. Kara Bruce (is / have / has) twenty-six years old, and she (study / studies) at the University of British Columbia. Every day, she (walk / walks) on Kitsilano beach. The beach (exist / exists) because some private citizens bought the land from Canadian Pacific Railway. There (is / are) some unique installations on that beach. For example, it (have / has) Canada's longest swimming pool. The outdoor pool, which (doesn't use / don't use) chlorine, (have / has) a saltwater system. In the summers, there (is / are) many sunbathers on the beach. Also, sailing (is / are) popular in Vancouver. However, sailing (cost / costs) a lot of money.

4. Vancouver is in an earthquake zone. The city (lie / lies) in the "Pacific Ring of Fire" which (include / includes) active volcanoes and shifting tectonic plates. According to experts, a major earthquake (is / are) "inevitable." However, almost nobody (worry / worries) about it. Most people (don't want / doesn't want) to live with constant fear. Nearly everybody (have / has) a good time in British Columbia.

EXERCISE 3   CONJUGATE VERBS

The simple present is often used to narrate a story. Read the paragraphs and add –s or –es to verbs that follow third-person-singular subjects. There are fifteen verbs to conjugate, not including the example.

1. One of the most popular books in recent years is Stephenie Meyer's novel, *Twilight*. Bella Swan, the main character, move [moves] to Forks, Washington. She stay [stays] with her father, and she go [goes] to the local school. She meet [meets] Edward, a quiet boy with pale skin. Nobody like [likes] the boy because he do [does] strange things. For instance, at school, he never eat [eats].

2. Soon, Bella fall [falls] in love with the quiet outsider. Over time, Bella discover [discovers] that Edward is a vampire. He and his family have strong values and never drink human blood. Instead, they kill small animals. The novel have [has] some surprising twists and turns.

3. *Twilight* follow [follows] a Gothic literary tradition. Many horror novels describe a creature who drink [drinks] human blood. Usually, the vampire have [has] pale skin and look [looks] attractive. He is always very old, yet he remain [remains] young and beautiful forever. The books appeal to our human desire for eternal youth, and the romance help [helps] the story.

SIMPLE PRESENT: QUESTION AND NEGATIVE FORMS

Remember to add *do* or *does* to question and negative forms. Use the base form of the main verb. **Exception:** When the verb is *be*, don't add another auxiliary.

Most verbs: When **does** the flight **leave**? We **don't need** our passports.

Be: Where **is** my laptop? My laptop **isn't** in my suitcase.

EXERCISE 4 SIMPLE PRESENT QUESTION AND NEGATIVE FORMS

PART A

Circle the subject in each sentence. Write *do*, *does*, or a form of *be* in the spaces provided. Then write the contracted negative verb.

> **EXAMPLE:** Does (England) have two capital cities? No, it _doesn't have_ two capital cities.

1. _____Does_____ (England) have a president? No, the country _____doesn't have_____ a president. It has a prime minister.

2. _____Do_____ British (citizens) use the euro? No, they _____don't use_____ the euro. They use the British pound.

3. _____Are_____ the (subways) open all night? No, they _____aren't_____ open all night. They close each night for several hours.

4. _____Do_____ (people) smoke in restaurants? No, they _____don't smoke_____ in restaurants. It is illegal.

5. _____Is_____ (it) expensive to visit the British museum? No, it _____isn't_____ expensive. The museum is free.

6. _____Do_____ Scottish (citizens) speak German? No, they _____don't speak_____ German. They speak English.

London Bridge

PART B

Make negative questions. Add *not* to the auxiliary.

> **EXAMPLE:** _____Don't_____ you like to travel?

7. _____Isn't_____ the coastline beautiful?

8. Why _____doesn't_____ Helen learn French?

9. Why _____don't_____ you go there?

10. Why _____doesn't_____ Ted like London?

11. _____Aren't_____ the gardens beautiful?

12. _____Don't_____ you have a passport?

QUESTION WORDS

The following words are used to form questions.

Who refers to a person
    Who are you?
    Who do you work with?

What refers to a thing.
    What is in that soup?

When refers to a time.
    When do you wake up?

Where refers to a place.
    Where do you live?

Why refers to a reason.
    Why is he busy?

How refers to a method or degree.
    How did you make this?
    How hot is it?

How long refers to a period of time.
    How long is the movie?

How far refers to a distance.
    How far is Tokyo from here?

How often refers to the frequency of an activity.
    How often do you see a doctor?

How much and **how many** refer to an amount of something.
    How much does it cost?
    How many cars are there?

How old refers to age.
    How old is Richie?

TIP

When the Main Verb Is *Do*

Do is both a verb and an auxiliary. When the main verb is *do* or *does*, you must still add an auxiliary to question and negative forms.

	auxiliary	verb
He **does** his homework.	When **does** he usually **do** his homework?	

EXERCISE 5   INFORMATION QUESTIONS

Write the questions in the spaces provided. The exact answers to the questions are in bold.

    EXAMPLE: She lives **in Nairobi.**   <u>Where does she live?</u>

1. Kenya has **two** official languages.

    <u>How many official languages does Kenya have?</u>

2. Natalia lives in Kenya **because she works for the United Nations**.

    <u>Why does Natalia live in Kenya?</u>

3. The capital of Kenya is **Nairobi.**

    <u>What is the capital of Kenya?</u>

4. The photo depicts **Kenya's wild gazelles.**

    <u>What does the photo depict?</u>

Amboseli, Kenya

→

5. She visits her parents **every year**.

How often does she visit her parents?

_____

6. She stays in Canada for **two weeks**.

How long does she stay in Canada?

_____

7. She does **research on AIDS** for the UN.

What does she do for the UN?

_____

8. Many Canadians work in **Kenya**.

Where do many Canadians work?

_____

FREQUENCY ADVERBS

Frequency adverbs define the frequency of an action and can appear mid-sentence.

never	rarely	seldom	sometimes	usually	often	always
			occasionally	generally	frequently	

⟵──────────────────────────────────────⟶

0%   100% of the time

Place frequency adverbs in the following positions:

– after *be*	She <u>is</u> **often** tired.
– before all other simple-tense verbs	He **usually** <u>arrives</u> on time.
– after auxiliary verbs	She <u>can</u> **always** help us.
– after the subject in question forms	Does <u>she</u> **occasionally** work late?

EXERCISE 6 PLACING FREQUENCY ADVERBS

PART A

Using an arrow, indicate where each frequency adverb should be placed.

EXAMPLE: (sometimes) Fears are ⌃ difficult to overcome.

1. (always) Some people are ⌃ afraid in airplanes.

2. (rarely) Airplanes ⌃ explode in the sky.

3. (often) I ⌃ take the bus or train instead of flying.

4. (rarely) The average passenger is ⌃ nervous on a plane.

5. (sometimes) People can ⌃ overreact to news reports about plane crashes.

6. (ever) Do you ⌃ worry about being in a plane accident?

7. (never) Most frequent flyers ⌃ worry about plane crashes.

8. (usually) My boyfriend and I are ⌃ very comfortable in airplanes.

PART B

Underline and correct the errors in the placement of the frequency adverbs. Write C next to correct sentences.

is often
EXAMPLE: Mr. Rae <u>often is</u> in an airplane.

often exaggerates
9. The media <u>exaggerates often</u> the risks of air travel.

is rarely
10. Air travel <u>rarely is</u> dangerous.

11. We usually take the train. C

seldom have
12. Planes <u>have seldom</u> accidents.

Students can practise spelling progressive verbs on the Companion Website.

EXERCISE 7 SPELLING PRESENT PROGRESSIVE FORMS

Write the following verbs in their progressive form. (If necessary, refer to the spelling rules on page 16.)

EXAMPLE: ask ___asking___

1. shop ___shopping___
2. carry ___carrying___
3. study ___studying___
4. write ___writing___
5. plan ___planning___
6. save ___saving___

7. try ___trying___
8. play ___playing___
9. begin ___beginning___
10. happen ___happening___
11. open ___opening___
12. develop ___developing___

Visit the Companion Website for more practice spelling present tense verbs.

TIP

Non-Progressive Verbs

Some verbs are not used in the progressive form because they express a perception, preference, state, or possession. For a list of some non-progressive verbs, see page 16.

loves
Kevin is hiking on a mountain. He ~~is loving~~ nature.

Answers will vary.

EXERCISE 8 PROGRESSIVE AND NON-PROGRESSIVE VERBS

Look at each photo and write two sentences using the verbs indicated. One sentence must be in the simple present and one in the present progressive. Remember that some verbs are non-progressive. See page 16 for a list of some non-progressive verbs.

EXAMPLE: (take photo, see an eagle)

He **is taking** a photo.

He **sees** an eagle.

1. (argue, not trust)

They are arguing.

She doesn't trust him.

2. (resemble each other, smile)

They resemble each other.

They are smiling.

3. (hold a fish, not smell good)

She is holding a fish.

It does not smell good.

4. (like each other, hug)

They like each other.

They are hugging.

5. (ride, own)

They are riding a motorcycle.

They own a motorcycle.

SIMPLE PRESENT OR PRESENT PROGRESSIVE?

Review the difference between the simple present and the present progressive.

Simple Present	**Present Progressive**
The action is a general truth, fact, habit, or custom.	The action is happening now.

Kevin **works** as a doctor.
He **drives** to work every day.

Right now, he **is taking** a photo.
These days, he **is travelling** in Kenya.

EXERCISE 9 SIMPLE PRESENT OR PRESENT PROGRESSIVE

In each sentence, underline the correct verb and then identify if the action is a fact, a habit, or is happening now.

Write *F* beside any facts, *H* beside any habits, or *N* beside actions that are happening now.

EXAMPLES: Sharks always (<u>live</u> / are living) in water.	F
He usually (<u>drives</u> / is driving) to work.	H
He (watches / <u>is watching</u>) a movie.	N

Machu Picchu

1. Marco usually (travel / <u>travels</u> / is travelling) with his girlfriend.   H

2. These days, they (visit / visits / <u>are visiting</u>) Peru.   N

3. In Peru, most people (<u>speak</u> / speaks / are speaking) Spanish.   F

4. Right now, Marco's girlfriend (speak / speaks / <u>is speaking</u>) to him.   N

5. At this moment, they (look / looks / <u>are looking</u>) at the ruins in Machu Picchu.   N

6. Alicia usually (take / <u>takes</u> / is taking) a lot of photos.   H

7. Alicia (take / takes / <u>is taking</u>) a photograph of an old stone wall.   N

8. The site (contain / <u>contains</u> / is containing) many ancient buildings.   F

PRESENT PROGRESSIVE: QUESTION AND NEGATIVE FORMS

In question forms, the verb *be* acts as an auxiliary and goes before the subject.
In negative forms, just place *not* after the verb *be*.

Is Mark **working** right now? He **is not relaxing**.

EXERCISE 10 QUESTION FORMS

Write questions using the simple present or the present progressive.
The exact answer to each question is in bold.

EXAMPLE: Omar is visiting **a museum**.   What is Omar visiting?

1. Omar is visiting Russia **because the historical architecture is beautiful**.

   Why is Omar visiting Russia?

2. **Yes**, he is staying in a small hotel.

   Is he staying in a small hotel?

3. His hotel costs **$40** per night.

   How much does his hotel cost per night?

4. He wants to see **St. Basil's Cathedral**.

   What does he want to see?

5. Omar is **resting** now.

   What is Omar doing now?

St. Basil's Cathedral,
Moscow

TIP

Use the Base Form after *Do, Does,* and *To*

Remember to use the base form of verbs that follow *do, does,* and *to* (infinitive form).

   swim   **laugh**
Does she ~~swims~~? She likes to ~~laughs~~.

EXERCISE 11 IDENTIFY ERRORS

Underline and correct fifteen errors in the next paragraphs, not including the example.

1. Many people ~~enjoys~~ [enjoy] extreme travel adventures. Graham Hughes, who ~~are~~ [is] thirty-one
   years old, wants to ~~visits~~ [visit] every sovereign state in the world without flying in an
   airplane. He hopes to break a world record. Currently, he [is] ~~visiting~~ his 183rd country.

2. Hughes usually ~~travel~~ [travels] on trains, buses, and boats. Occasionally he ~~is riding~~ [rides] a
   bike. Often, someone ~~give~~ [gives] him a lift. These days, he is in Australia. To save
   money, he usually ~~sleep~~ [sleeps] on people's couches. Right now, he ~~stay~~ [is staying] with a couple
   in Sydney. Hughes, who is British, ~~need~~ [needs] a visa to stay in Australia. He doesn't
   ~~needs~~ [need] a visa when he comes to Canada.

3. Why Hughes is trying to break a world record? What
    (is Hughes)

    do he hope to accomplish? He wants to raise money
    (does)

    for "Water Aid." It is an organization that provide
    (provides)

    access to safe water and sanitation. Apparently, there

    is millions of children who die every year because
    (are)

    they do'nt have access to clean water and sanitation.
    (don't)

↺ UNIT Review

Answer the following questions. If you don't know an answer, go back and review the appropriate section.

1. When do you put an –s or –es on a verb?

    When the subject is third person singular, or when the subject is *he*, *she*, or *it*

2. What is the difference between the following sentences?

    She is talking loudly. _The action is happening now._

    She talks loudly. _The action is a fact or habit._

3. Underline and correct the verb error and/or word placement error in each sentence. Then explain why the sentence is incorrect.

    a) Jay dream sometimes about flying. _sometimes dreams_

      Frequency adverbs go before simple-tense verbs. *Dream* requires an *s* because it follows

      a third-person-singular subject.

    b) Every summer, he is swimming in a lake. _swims_

      The sentence describes a habit.

    c) Right now, he not laughing. _is not laughing_

      Use a form of *be* before –*ing*.

    d) His laptop don't works very well. _doesn't work_

      The –*s* is added to the auxiliary, not to the main verb.

4. Write yes/no questions.

    EXAMPLE: They are fighting. _Are they fighting?_

    a) It is raining. _Is it raining?_

    b) She needs an umbrella. _Does she need an umbrella?_

    c) They are wet. _Are they wet?_

    d) They work together. _Do they work together?_

Need more practice?
Visit the Companion Website and try other present tense exercises.

Final Review

You can use the Final Review as a test. There are fifteen answers in Part A, and five answers each in Parts B and C, for a total of twenty-five points. You can find additional practice exercises and testing material on the Companion Website.

PART A

Fill in the blanks with the correct present tense verb.

EXAMPLE: Right now, I (sit) __am sitting__ on a bench in Sydney, Australia.

1. Travelling usually (require) __requires__ money, time, and energy. Right now, my sister and I (stay) __are staying__ in Sydney, Australia. Usually, we (have, not) __don't have__ a lot of time to relax. But at this moment, we (sit) __are sitting__ on a bench at Sydney Harbour. Right now, everyone (take) __is taking__ photos of the Sydney Opera House.

2. The Opera House is a World Heritage Site. There (be) __are__ over one million white granite tiles on the roof. More than seven million people (visit) __visit__ the Opera House each year.

3. There (be) __are__ many unusual animals in Australia. Arlene is from Australia, and she (like, not) __doesn't like__ kangaroos. The animals (run) __run__ across highways, and they often (cause) __cause__ accidents. How often (drivers, see) __do drivers see__ kangaroos on public highways?

4. Arlene often (swim) __swims__ in the ocean. Sometimes great white sharks (approach) __approach__ the coast, so everyone (have) __has__ to be careful.

PART B

Correct five errors in present tense verbs.

          enjoy
EXAMPLE: We ~~enjoys~~ Australia.

5. Right now, a shark is ~~swim~~ (swimming) near the beach.
   Look! People ~~is~~ (are) running out of the water.
   Generally, nobody ~~is knowing~~ (knows) when a shark will attack, but people should relax. There ~~is~~ (are) only about seven serious shark attacks each year. ~~Do you are~~ (Are you) afraid of sharks?

28 | AVENUES 2 | English Grammar

PART C

Write questions for the sentences below. The exact answers are in bold.

> **EXAMPLE:** She is visiting **the Sydney Opera House**.   <u>What is she visiting?</u>

6. The most popular attraction is **the Opera House**.

   What is the most popular attraction?

7. Arlene works **near the harbour**.

   Where does Arlene work?

8. Airplane tickets to Australia cost **$2150**.

   How much do airplane tickets to Australia cost?

9. The flight takes **21 hours**.

   How long does the flight take?

10. The captain is discussing **the weather** right now.

    What is the captain discussing right now?

SPEAKING AND WRITING

Students can do the writing exercise on a separate sheet of paper. Once students have finished, ask them to exchange their writing and peer edit for the correct use of verbs.

Interview a Partner

Work with a partner and find five things that you have in common. Think about common interests, friends, histories, bad habits, and experiences. Then think of three major differences between you and your partner. Write a text showing how you are similar and different.

_____

_____

_____

_____

_____

_____

_____

_____

_____

_____

_____

_____

_____

_____

Past Tenses

Preview

WHAT ARE PAST TENSES?

The **simple past** indicates that an action was completed at a definite time in the past.
The **past progressive** indicates that an action was in progress at a specific past time.

  past progressive   simple past
Yesterday, I **was driving** on the highway when I **saw** an accident.

IRREGULAR VERB PUZZLE

Determine the simple past form of the verbs. Then highlight them in the puzzle.
The verbs could be written in any direction (up, down, sideways, or diagonally).

become	cut	fall	keep	say	take
begin	dig	feel	know	sell	teach
break	do	give	leave	sing	tell
build	drink	go	lose	sit	think
buy	~~drive~~	have	make	speak	write
choose	eat	hide	meet	spend	

After you finish highlighting the verbs, put the remaining letters in the spaces below to reveal the secret sentence. (Choose letters horizontally, moving from the top row down.) The secret sentence means that money does not buy happiness. What is the secret sentence?

W T D R A N K F E L T H L
E W R O T E E G S O L D O
N B E C A M E M A D E B S
T E T A U G H T M V S C T
T T D B R O K E E S E H H
S I I N G D B B T P K O T
S A D I N R U E L E N S H
C I I F S O I G E N E E O
U F A D A V L A H T W H U
T S E R N E T N E A F I G
O O A L G L E F T R D D H
L E O T L E S P O K E P T
D U G K A T E B O U G H T

T h e _ b e s t
t h i n g s
i n _ l i f e
a r e _ f r e e .

Past Tenses: Forms and Usage

The **simple past** indicates that an action was completed at a definite time in the past. The **past progressive** indicates that an action was in progress when another action happened or interrupted the first action.

Last night, I **was cooking** when the fire **started**.

Last night		**Now**
the fire **started** (simple past)		

I **was cooking**
(past progressive)

	SIMPLE PAST	PAST PROGRESSIVE
FORM	Regular verbs: looked, wanted, talked … Irregular verbs: ate, broke, had, saw …	I, He, She, It was + <u>verb</u> + –ing. You, We, They were + <u>verb</u> + –ing.
USAGE	The **simple past** indicates that an action was completed at a definite time in the past. Last week, Kaya **bought** new boots. **Keywords:** ago, yesterday, last week, when I was a child, many years ago, once upon a time, in the 1990s, in 2012 …	The **past progressive** shows that an action was in progress at a specific past time. It can also show that a past action was interrupted. Yesterday at 1 a.m., we **were sleeping**. (specific past time) While I **was eating** lunch, the phone rang. (interrupted action) **Keywords:** as, when, while, during, at 4 a.m., at noon …
QUESTION	Put *did* before the subject. Use the base form of the verb. **Did** Julie **travel** last year? **Exception:** *be* **Was** Julie late? **Were** you angry?	Put *be* before the subject. **Was** I **bothering** you during lunch? **Were** they **sleeping** at 9 a.m.?
NEGATIVE	Add *did* with *not*. Julie **did not** travel last year. (didn't) **Exception:** *be* They were **not** late, and I was **not** alone. (weren't) (wasn't)	Add *not*. I was **not** bothering you during lunch. (wasn't) They were **not** sleeping at 9 a.m. (weren't)

SIMPLE PAST: SPELLING REGULAR PAST VERBS

There are both **regular** and **irregular** simple past tense verbs. **Regular simple past** verbs take –ed and generally don't appear on verb lists (such as the one on page 153) because of their standard form.

LAST LETTER(S) OF VERB	EXAMPLE	–ED FORM	RULE
silent –e	smile	smil**ed**	Just add –d.
consonant + –y	study	stud**ied**	Change the –y to –ied.
vowel + –y	stay	stay**ed**	Just add –ed.
consonant-vowel-consonant (in one-syllable verbs)	shop	sho**pped**	Double the last letter and add –ed. **Exception**: words that end in –x or –w (fix ▶ fixed).
consonant-vowel-consonant (in verbs of more than one syllable)	re**fer** o**mit**	refe**rred** omi**tted**	Double the last letter when the verb ends in a stressed syllable, and add –ed.*
	BUT		
	open **hap**pen	open**ed** happen**ed**	If the verb doesn't end in a stressed syllable, just add –ed.

* To know which syllable is stressed, refer to your dictionary or visit an online dictionary. A heavy black mark may precede the stressed syllable, or the stressed syllable may be written in bold font.

IRREGULAR SIMPLE PAST VERBS

Some simple past verbs do not end in any specific letter. For a list of irregular simple past verbs, see Appendix 3 on page 153.

Practice

EXERCISE 1 REGULAR PAST TENSE VERBS

Write the past tense form of the following verbs. The spelling rules are explained above.

EXAMPLE: watch ___watched___

1. carry ___carried___
2. stay ___stayed___
3. deny ___denied___
4. employ ___employed___
5. study ___studied___

6. plan ___planned___
7. rain ___rained___
8. open ___opened___
9. prefer ___preferred___
10. question ___questioned___

Visit the Companion Website for more practice spelling past tense verbs.

TIP

There Was and *There Were*

Remember the differences between *there was* and *there were*.

There was one thing.   **There were** two or more things.

EXERCISE 2 WAS AND *WERE*

Write the present or past tense form of *be* in the spaces provided. Use the affirmative or negative form of the verb.

EXAMPLE: The singer _was_ alone on the stage.

Melissa Auf der Maur

1. Melissa Auf der Maur _____was_____ born in Montreal. Where _____were_____ you born?

2. When Auf der Maur _____was_____ two years old, she lived with her mother, in Africa. They visited safari parks. At the first park they visited, there _____was_____ a snake, and there _____were_____ many elephants.

3. Her parents (not) _____weren't_____ typical. Her mother (not) _____wasn't_____ like most other mothers.

4. Linda Gaboriau, Auf der Maur's mother, (not) _____wasn't_____ an ordinary housewife. She _____was_____ Montreal's first female disc jockey, and she became an award-winning translator.

5. Auf der Maur _____was_____ with the band Hole for five years. At her first concert with the band in England, there _____was_____ a really big stage. There _____were_____ many people in the audience.

PAST VERSUS *PASSED*

Some people confuse *past* and *passed*. **Past** is a noun that means "in a previous time; before now."

She has many secrets in her **past**. Her mistakes are in the **past**.

Passed is the past tense of the verb *pass*, which has many meanings. In the first example below, it means "went by." In the second example, it means "to complete successfully."

Many days **passed**, and the nights got shorter.
She **passed** her exams.

EXERCISE 3 AFFIRMATIVE AND NEGATIVE FORMS

Fill in the blanks with simple past verbs. Use either the affirmative or the negative form.

EXAMPLE: Gabrielle "Coco" Chanel (have, not) _didn't have_ children.

1. Gabrielle Chanel was born in 1883 and she (die) _____died_____ in 1971. She (grow, not) _____didn't grow_____ up in luxury. When she was twelve years old, her mother (fall) _____fell_____ ill.

Then her mother (pass) _____ passed _____ away, and her

father (leave) _____ left _____ the family. He (want, not)

_____ didn't want _____ to raise his five children alone, so he sent

them to live with relatives.

2. Chanel (become) _____ became _____ a singer in 1905,

and she (keep, not) _____ didn't keep _____ the name Gabrielle.

She adopted the name Coco instead. Then, in 1908, Chanel (be, not)

_____ wasn't _____ happy as a singer. She (prefer)

_____ preferred _____ to design hats. She (have, not)

_____ didn't have _____ any money, so she borrowed money

to open a boutique. At first, there (be, not) _____ wasn't _____

much interest in her clothing.

3. She (like, not) _____ didn't like _____ the frilly clothing of that era,

so she created simple, boyish designs. In the 1920s, women (wear, not)

_____ didn't wear _____ corsets anymore. Instead, they (choose)

_____ chose _____ to wear simple dresses like the ones

designed by Coco Chanel.

4. Before 1923, there (be, not) _____ weren't _____ any perfumes

with designers' names. Chanel (be) _____ was _____ the first

designer to link a perfume with the name of a fashion house. She created

Chanel No. 5 perfume. She (expect, not) _____ didn't expect _____

the product to be so successful.

Coco Chanel

SUBJECT QUESTIONS

When using *who*, *what* and *how many* to ask about the subject of a question, you
don't need an auxiliary. (An auxiliary is a helping verb such as *do*, *does*, or *did*.)

Ben called Anna.   **Their house** had blue walls.   **Fifty** people were there.
↑   ↑   ↑
Who called Anna?   **What** had blue walls?   **How many people**
                                                                       were there?

When *who(m)*,* *what* and *how many* ask about the <u>object</u> of a question, you must
add an auxiliary to the question.

Ben called **Anna**.   Their house had **blue walls**.   She had **fifty** friends.
     └───────────↑   └──────────────↑   └──────────↑
Who(m) did Ben call?   **What did** their house have?   **How many friends did**
                                                               she have?

* *Whom* is used in formal and academic English. In informal English, it is acceptable to use *who*.

EXERCISE 4 QUESTIONS

Change the following sentences into questions. The answer to each question is
.in bold.

> **EXAMPLE:** Natalie Portman's first film was **the French movie *The Professional***.
> *What was Natalie Portman's first film?*

1. Natalie Portman lived in Israel **for eight years**.

　　How long did Natalie Portman live in Israel?

2. She began her film career **in 1994**.

　　When did she begin her film career?

3. **Luc Besson** was her first director.

　　Who was her first director?

4. Her first movie was **in France**.

　　Where was her first movie?

5. ***Black Swan*** was strange.

　　What was strange? / Which movie was strange?

6. Portman **played a ballet dancer** in *Black Swan*.

　　What did Portman do in *Black Swan*?

7. **Critics** praised Portman's dancing.

　　Who praised Portman's dancing?

8. Sarah Lane complained **because she was the real dancer in *Black Swan***.

　　Why did Sarah Lane complain?

USE THE BASE FORM AFTER *DID* AND *TO*

Remember to use the base form of verbs that follow *did* and *to* (infinitive form).

　　change　　　　　　　　　　　　　**study**
Did he ~~changed~~ his appearance? Ellis wanted to ~~studied~~ anthropology.

EXERCISE 5 IDENTIFY ERRORS

Underline and correct the past tense errors. If the sentence is correct, write *C* in
the space provided.

> **EXAMPLE:** In the past, did you <u>watched</u> *The Simpsons*?　　watch

1. In 1985, Nina Matsumoto <u>is</u> born in Vancouver.　　was

2. A few years ago, she wanted to <u>became</u>
a manga artist.　　become

3. In 2007, she <u>choosed</u> the online name
"Space Coyote."　　chose

→

4. She put one of her drawings on DeviantArt.com.   _____C_____

5. Why did she <u>transformed</u> the Simpsons into "anime" characters?   _____transform_____

6. At that time, she <u>don't expected</u> a big reaction.   _____didn't expect_____

7. There <u>was</u> millions of viewers on the website.   _____were_____

8. Matt Groening and other famous artists tried to <u>met</u> with her.   _____meet_____

9. Why <u>the response was</u> so intense?   _____was the response_____

10. The Internet <u>maked</u> her famous.   _____made_____

EXERCISE 6 **REVIEW THE SIMPLE PAST**

Fill in the blanks below with the simple past form of each verb. Note that the verb may be regular or irregular.

EXAMPLE: Marc Chagall (leave) <u>left</u> his hometown in 1906.

1. In Russia in the early 20th century, Jewish parents (send) _____sent_____ their children to Jewish religious schools because Russian schools (accept, not) _____did not accept_____ them. Iconic artist Marc Chagall, from the small Russian town of Vitebsk, (face) _____faced_____ many obstacles on his road to success.

2. Chagall (grow) _____grew_____ up in a strict Hasidic Jewish family. He (begin) _____began_____ his art education when he (be) _____was_____ thirteen years old. He later attended an art school in Vitebsk, but he (like, not) _____didn't like_____ the school. The teachers (teach) _____taught_____ art in a very rigid way. He (leave) _____left_____ school and (go) _____went_____ to St. Petersburg when he (be) _____was_____ nineteen years old. Jewish artists at the time (have) _____had_____ two options to try to become artists: they could hide their roots, or they could embrace them and make them part of their art. Chagall (make) _____made_____ the decision to embrace his roots.

Marc Chagall

3. What (he, do) _____ did he do _____ after leaving his hometown?

In the early 1920s, Chagall (go) _____ went _____ to France

and was one of the most respected artists of the modernist movement.

However, in the early 1940s, with the rise of Nazism in Germany, Chagall

(have) _____ had _____ many problems. Some Nazi troops (try)

_____ tried _____ to arrest Chagall, but an American journalist

saved him. During World War II, why (be) _____ were _____ some

people so intolerant?

PAST HABITS AND SERIES OF PAST ACTIONS

Use the *past progressive* to describe a past action that was in progress. Do not overuse the past progressive tense. Never use the past progressive tense to talk about past habits or a series of past actions.

Past habit: Renoir ~~was drawing~~ **drew** pictures of his friends when he was younger.

Series of past actions: When she was young, she ~~was painting~~ **painted** pictures, ~~was studying~~ **studied** music, and ~~was learning~~ **learned** a second language.

EXERCISE 7 SIMPLE PAST AND PAST PROGRESSIVE

Fill in the spaces with either the simple past or the past progressive verb forms. (Refer to the explanations about the two tenses at the beginning of this unit.)

1.   Concepts of beauty are not universal. On Saturday at 2 p.m., while Angie (visit) _____ was visiting _____ a gallery with her friend Rob, they had an argument. Angie (love) _____ loved _____ the artwork on display and she (think) _____ thought _____ that the paintings (be) _____ were _____ beautiful. However, while she (express) _____ was expressing _____ her opinion, Rob (cough) _____ coughed _____. Then Rob (say) _____ said _____, "I hate modern art."

2.   Often, artists are not appreciated during their lifetimes. Van Gogh (sell, not) _____ didn't sell _____ many paintings. His work (be, not) _____ wasn't _____ popular, and many people (laugh) _____ laughed _____ at his artwork.

3. In the 1990s, art lovers (pay) _____ paid _____ millions
   of dollars for Van Gogh artworks. In fact, at one auction, while people (bid)
   _____ were bidding _____ on Van Gogh's *Portrait of Dr. Gachet*, the crowd
   suddenly gasped: an art collector (be) _____ was _____ ready
   to spend $82.5 million for the painting.

EXERCISE 8 IDENTIFY PAST PROGRESSIVE ERRORS

Underline and correct six past progressive errors in the selection.

EXAMPLE: When James Cameron was young, he <u>was loving</u> to make movies.
                                                          loved

James Cameron

1. James Cameron grew up in Chippawa, Ontario. In 1973,
   Cameron went to a California university to study pure
   sciences. Often while he <u>sitting</u> in class, he drew pictures
   (was)
   in his books. He dropped out of his program, and then
   he <u>was taking</u> a job as a truck driver. One day in 1977,
   (took)
   while he <u>watching</u> the movie *Star Wars*, he had an idea.
   (was)
   He realized that he could integrate science and art.

2. Cameron started to make special effects for the movie *Piranha II*. While the
   technicians <u>was</u> making some special effects, Cameron had an idea about
   (were)
   robots. After that, he <u>was write</u> a story about robots that take over the world.
   (wrote)
   A production company hired Cameron to direct his movie, *The Terminator*. Then,
   in 2008, Cameron directed *Avatar*. While the actors <u>was</u> filming a jungle scene,
   (were)
   a large light crashed to the ground. Luckily, nobody was hurt.

EXERCISE 9 QUESTION FORMS

Write a question under each statement. The exact answer is in bold.

EXAMPLE: Kayla watched the movie **last night**. <u>When did Kayla watch the movie?</u>

1. Cameron filmed *Avatar* **in 2008**.
   When did Cameron film *Avatar*?

2. He was living in California **in 2008**.
   Where was he living in 2008?

3. **Yes**, the movie was popular.

   Was the movie popular? _____

4. The movie cost **$250 million**.

   How much did the movie cost? _____

5. The actor **was eating** when he heard the news.

   What was the actor doing when he heard the news? _____

6. People loved the movie **because the 3-D effects were special**.

   Why did people love t he movie? _____

AVOIDING TENSE INCONSISTENCIES

If you start to tell a story, do not shift tenses unless the time frame really changes.

                                                     happened

Last Saturday, I **walked** under a ladder. Suddenly, bad things ~~happen~~.

TIP

Would and *Could*

When you tell a story about a past event, use *would* instead of *will*, and *could* instead of *can*.

                        would   **could**

In my childhood, I knew that I ~~will~~ leave home when I ~~can~~ afford it.

EXERCISE 10 IDENTIFY TENSE SHIFTS

Underline and correct ten tense inconsistencies. Put the entire story in the past tense.

1. One day, a notorious pirate named Blackbeard retreated to

   Teach Cove, his favourite hideaway. He will [would] steal from any

   other ship when he was at sea. Robert Maynard, of the Royal

   Navy, wanted to capture Blackbeard. The pirate sailed for

   months until he can't [couldn't] sail anymore. Finally, Blackbeard decides [decided]

   to stop and fight his pursuer. Maynard has [had] hundreds of troops

   at his disposal. Blackbeard can [could] fight really well, but Maynard →

had better weapons. It took five gunshots to finally kill the pirate. Maynard
removes Blackbeard's head to be sure he was actually dead.
<u>removes</u> ~~removed~~ (removed written above removes)

2. Later, Maynard's crew members ~~will~~ <u>will</u> sometimes see an apparition that looked
would (would written above will)

like a headless body in the water. They believed that the pirate was a ghost,

and that he <u>can</u> appear behind the ship. They thought that the pirate <u>is</u> looking
could (could written above can) — *was* (was written above is)

for his head. The tough sailors became scared. Some crew members <u>can't</u>
couldn't (couldn't written above can't)

sleep at night and others had nightmares. They only found peace when their

ship returned to shore.

↻ UNIT Review

Answer the following questions. If you don't know an answer, go back and
review the appropriate section.

1. When do you use the past progressive?
   When an action was in progress at a specific past time or when a past action was interrupted.

2. Correct the verb errors in the sentences below. Then explain why the
   sentences are incorrect.
   a) Every day, I was playing soccer.   played
      The past progressive isn't used for repeated past actions.

   b) Did you finished your meal?   finish
      Use the base form of verbs that follow *did*.

   c) Last night, I wanted to talked with you.   talk
      Use the base form of verbs after *to*.

3. Write the question and negative forms of the following sentences.
   a) She turned on the radio.
      Question: Did she turn on the radio?
      Negative: She didn't turn on the radio.

   b) They were sleeping when the fire started.
      Question: Were they sleeping when the fire started?
      Negative: They weren't sleeping when the fire started.

   c) He did his homework.
      Question: Did he do his homework?
      Negative: He didn't do his homework.

Need more
practice?
Visit the Companion Website
and try additional exercises.

Final Review

PART A

Fill in the blanks with the correct verb tense. Use either the simple past or the past progressive.

1. The British artist Banksy (grow) _____ grew _____ up in Bristol, England. When he (be) _____ was _____ fourteen years old, he began to spray-paint graffiti on walls and buildings. One day, while he (hide) _____ was hiding _____ from the police, he noticed the stencilled lettering on the police cruiser. He (want, not) _____ didn't want _____ the police to catch him.

2. Banksy (begin) _____ began _____ to use stencils so he could do his graffiti more quickly. Some of his first stencils (be) _____ were _____ comic depictions of police officers. In 1994, while he (paint) _____ was painting _____ an image of children hugging missiles, the police almost caught him.

3. In 2000, some British officials (be, not) _____ weren't _____ happy with Banksy. They called his work "vandalism." But that year, many ordinary citizens (become) _____ became _____ admirers of the artist. They (take) _____ took _____ photos of Banksy's street art and followed his work.

4. In the early 2000s, Banksy's fame increased, but he (want, not) _____ didn't want _____ to be recognized. He (have) _____ had _____ to be more careful. What (he, do) _____ did he do _____? He did elaborate stunts.

5. In 2005, Banksy (copy) _____ copied _____ one of the paintings in Monet's "Water Lilies" series, but he put old shopping carts in the water. He put the painting on the wall of London's Tate gallery. Nobody (see) _____ saw _____ him do it.

You can ask students to complete the final review and then detach this page. In the student books, pages are perforated.

PART B

Write questions for the following sentences. The answers are in bold.

EXAMPLE: Banksy painted graffiti **in Toronto**. <u>Where did Banksy paint graffiti?</u>

6. Banksy went to Los Angeles **in 2006**.
   <u>When did Banksy go to Los Angeles?</u>

7. He did a political act **in Disneyland**.
   <u>Where did he do a political act?</u>

8. He put **a blow-up doll** in the middle of the theme park.
   <u>What did he put in the middle of the theme park?</u>

9. The doll was wearing **the clothing of Guantanamo Bay detainees**.
   <u>What was the doll wearing?</u>

10. **Yes**, the Disney officials were angry.
    <u>Were the Disney officials angry?</u>

SPEAKING AND WRITING

Students can do the writing exercise on a separate sheet of paper. Once students have finished, ask them to exchange their writing and peer edit for the correct use of verbs.

Who Is It?

Work with a partner. First, describe a well-known person and explain why that person became famous. Give clues about the person, but do not say his or her name. Your partner must guess the person's name. Then write a short paragraph about the famous person that you or your partner described.

EXAMPLE: He was born in Nova Scotia.
He was captain of the Pittsburgh Penguins.
He scored the winning goal at the 2010 Olympic Games.

_____
_____
_____
_____
_____

UNIT 4

Future Tense

Preview

You can use the Preview activity to introduce the future tense. Students can then complete the unit in class or for homework.

WHAT IS THE FUTURE TENSE?

The **future tense** indicates that an action will occur at a future time. You can use *will* or *be going to* plus the verb.

In the future, I **will own** a house. I**'m going to live** in a big city.

YOUR FUTURE

Interview another student. Ask him or her what his or her future plans are. What will that person's life look like in five years? Write six questions. You can ask about relationships, transportation, work, health, and exercise. Then write your partner's answers. Write some things that person will and won't do. Be specific.

> **EXAMPLE:** Jordan will move to a better apartment.

Questions

1. _____
2. _____
3. _____
4. _____
5. _____
6. _____

Answers

1. _____
2. _____
3. _____
4. _____
5. _____
6. _____

Future Tense: Forms and Usage

The future tense indicates that an action will occur at a future time. You can use *will* or *be going to* plus the verb.

Next July, I **will move**. My friend **is going to move**, too.

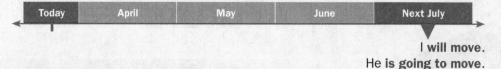

| Today | April | May | June | Next July |

I **will move**.
He **is going to move**.

Keywords: soon, later, tomorrow, the day after tomorrow, next week, next month, one day, in five years …

WILL AND BE GOING TO

Both *will* and *be going to* indicate a future action. You can use either form most of the time, but there are some small differences in meaning.

FUNCTION	FORM	EXAMPLE
Predictions	*will / be going to* + verb	We **will travel** next summer. We **are going to travel** next summer.
Spontaneous actions	*will* + verb	The phone is ringing. I **will answer** it.
Planned actions	*be going to* + verb	I'm **going to sell** my old television.

AFFIRMATIVE, QUESTION, AND NEGATIVE FORMS

Will

AFFIRMATIVE FORM	QUESTION FORM (Move *will* before the subject.)	NEGATIVE FORM (Add *not*.)
I He She It You We They } **will help.**	**Will** I he she it you we they } **help?**	I He She It You We They } **will not help.** (won't help.)

Be going to

AFFIRMATIVE FORM		QUESTION FORM (Move *be* before the subject.)			NEGATIVE FORM (Add *not*.)	
I	**am going to help.**	**Am**	I	**going to help?**	I	**am not going to help.**
He She It	**is going to help.**	**Is**	he she it	**going to help?**	He She It	**is not going to help.** (isn't going to help.)
You We They	**are going to help.**	**Are**	you we they	**going to help?**	You We They	**are not going to help** (aren't going to help.)

PRESENT TENSES CAN INDICATE THE FUTURE

Sometimes, present tense verbs indicate an event that will happen at a future time.

TENSE	MEANING	EXAMPLE
Simple present	scheduled event	The train **leaves** at noon.
Present progressive	previously planned event that will happen in the near future	We**'re taking** the bus tonight. The bus **is leaving** in ten minutes.

Practice

EXERCISE 1 IDENTIFY THE FUTURE TENSE

PART A

Underline eight future tense verbs in the following paragraph.

Albert Nerenberg is a "laughter expert." Next month, he <u>is going to travel</u> to Toronto to do a laughter workshop. People <u>will learn</u> about the benefits of good humour. Participants <u>will smile</u> at strangers. Nerenberg <u>is not going to spend</u> a lot of money. His hosts <u>are going to cover</u> his expenses. Workshop participants <u>won't stay</u> in hotels. They <u>will drive</u> to the event and then they <u>will return</u> home at night.

PART B

Now analyze the above paragraph.

1. What is the negative form of *will stay*?   won't stay

2. What is the negative form of *is going to spend*?   isn't going to spend

3. When there is a third-person-singular subject (*he, she, it*), do you need to add –s to *will*?   ☐ Yes ☑ No

4. Do you need to add –s to the verb that follows *will*?   ☐ Yes ☑ No

TIP

Will or *Be Going To*?

Use both *will* and *be going to* when you predict the future. For previously planned actions, use *be going to*. For spontaneous actions, use *will*.

Prediction: The population **will grow**. It **is going to explode**.
Planned: I found a job. I **am going to work** in Banff.
Spontaneous: The doorbell is ringing. I **will answer** it.

EXERCISE 2 WILL AND BE GOING TO

Read each sentence and explain why the underlined verb is *will* or *be going to*. (Future predictions, which can use *will* or *be going to*, are not included in this exercise.) Write *PL* if the action is planned, and *SP* if the action is spontaneous.

EXAMPLE: The dishes are dirty. I will wash them.   SP

1. I'm going to lose weight. I joined a health club.   PL

2. You don't have to pay the bill. I will pay it.   SP

3. We bought some tickets and we're going to see the show.   PL

4. I'll vacuum the rug. You don't have to do it.   SP

5. I quit my job because we're going to move.   PL

EXERCISE 3 FUTURE TENSE

Fill in the blanks with the future tense of the verb. Use the indicated future form. For negative verbs, use the contracted form. The first one has been done for you.

1. **(will)** In the future, some things (change) _____ will change _____ and some things (stay) _____ will stay _____ the same. What (robots, do) _____ will robots do _____? Maybe rich people (have) _____ will have _____ robotic servants. Perhaps robots (clean) _____ will clean _____ houses. Maybe in the future, people (need, not) _____ won't need _____ to cook.

2. **(be going to)** In the future, young people (still, pay) _____ _____ are still going to pay _____ taxes. However, perhaps there (be, not) _____ isn't going to be _____ enough money to pay for the increased costs to our health-care system. In the future, many people (work) _____ are going to work _____ until they are older than sixty-five. I (vote) _____ am going to vote _____ in the next election.

TIME CLAUSES

In sentences that indicate the future, use the present tense in time clauses. A time clause begins with a **time marker** such as *when*. Never use the future tense after these time markers:

after	before	until
as soon as	unless	when/whenever

The time marker can appear in the first or second part of the sentence.

time marker
Underline: When I **finish** college, I **will try to find** an interesting job.

time marker
Maya **will call** us as soon as she **arrives**.

EXERCISE 4 IDENTIFY TIME-CLAUSE ERRORS

Underline and correct the verb errors in the sentences below. Note that the time markers are in bold.

EXAMPLE: I will leave **as soon as** I ~~will finish~~ finish my work.

1. **When** Hamid ~~will find~~ finds a job, he will be very happy.

2. He will move out **as soon as** he ~~will graduate~~ graduates from college.

3. **After** Hamid ~~will leave~~ leaves, his parents will turn his bedroom into an office.

4. I will drive Hamid **unless** you ~~will want~~ want to.

5. **When** Hamid ~~will have~~ has his own apartment, he will feel independent.

EXERCISE 5 RECOGNIZE TIME MARKERS

Circle all the time markers and put the verbs in the present or future tense. Use *will* for future tense verbs.

EXAMPLE: The weather (get) _will get_ much worse (unless) we (use) _use_ fewer fossil fuels.

1. Many major newspapers (collapse) ___will collapse___ in the next twenty years (unless) they (change) ___change___ their business practices. In the future, newspapers (evolve) ___will evolve___ _____, or they will go bankrupt. Newspapers depend on advertising revenue. Today, younger people read their news online. (When) the older population (shrink) ___shrinks___, how (newspapers, afford) ___will newspapers afford___ their production costs? The decline in advertising revenue (continue) ___will continue___ in the near future. The North American newspaper industry has lost billions of dollars since 2007.

2. The solution is probably the Internet. In the future, I (read) ___will read___ _____ the news online. Next year, advertising revenue from the Internet (increase) ___will increase___. (When) newspapers (make) ___make___ more money from online advertising, maybe they (offer) ___will offer___ content exclusively online. In the future, (they, save) ___will they save___ money (as soon as) they (stop) ___stop___ printing and distributing newspapers?

2. The city of London ~~is gonna be~~ [is going to be] the first with a fleet of hydrogen-powered taxis.

The taxis ~~will works~~ [will work] without any fossil fuels. After London ~~will introduce~~ [introduces] the

taxis, maybe other countries will follow [C] England's decision. On the other

hand, maybe engineers ~~wont finish~~ [won't finish] the new taxis for a long time.

3. Toyota engineers ~~creating~~ [are creating] a zero-emissions car. The average person

~~isn't gonna have~~ [isn't going to have] enough money to buy it. Maybe Toyota will reduce [C] the price.

Are solar cars ~~is~~ [is̶] going to replace gasoline-powered cars? What will ~~be~~ the best

technology[be]?

ANSWERS

You can answer questions with short answers. Simply repeat the subject and the auxiliary. It isn't necessary to repeat the verb.

Will she leave soon?	Yes, **she will**.	OR	No, **she won't**.
Are they happy?	Yes, **they are**.	OR	No, **they aren't**.

EXERCISE 8 SHORT ANSWERS

Answer the following questions with short answers. The questions are in the present, past, or future tenses.

EXAMPLE: Will I be able to afford a house? Yes, I __will__. No, I __won't__.

1. Am I working right now?   Yes, __I am__.   No, __I'm not__.
2. Are we going to have a pension?   Yes, __we will__. No, __we won't__.
3. Are they going to buy computers?   Yes, __they are__. No, __they aren't__.
4. Will Ray retire at sixty-five?   Yes, __he will__. No, __he won't__.
5. Do they want a flying car?   Yes, __they do__. No, __they don't__.
6. Does Jay believe in climate change? Yes, __he does__. No, __he doesn't__.
7. Did she graduate?   Yes, __she did__. No, __she didn't__.
8. Will the future be better for us?   Yes, __it will__. No, __it won't__.

EXERCISE 9 PRESENT, PAST, AND FUTURE

Write the verb in the correct tense—present, past, or future—in the spaces provided. For negative verbs, use the contracted form.

EXAMPLE: Where (you, live) _do you live_ ?

1. Many years ago, doctors (use) _____used_____ herb therapies to treat sick

patients. In the past, doctors (know, not) _____didn't know_____ very much

about treating cancer. There (be, not) _____weren't_____ effective treatments

➜

in the 19th century. Now doctors (have) _____have_____ many treatment options. What (they, do) _____do they do_____ most often? Generally, doctors (treat) _____treat_____ patients using chemotherapy. However, the therapy (have) _____has_____ many serious side effects, and it is very unpleasant.

2. What types of medical care (there, be) _____will there be_____ in the future? Perhaps small medical robots (destroy) _____will destroy_____ bacteria and other germs.

3. In the future, medical companies (use) _____will use_____ nanorobots. The little robots (attach) _____will attach_____ to cancerous cells. Tiny machines (kill) _____will kill_____ individual cancer cells. Maybe future cancer patients (need, not) _____won't need_____ extensive chemotherapy.

4. Of course, people (want, not) _____don't want_____ to get sick. But maybe in the future, people (suffer, not) _____won't suffer_____ from terminal diseases. If scientists (find) _____find_____ a cure for cancer, maybe people's lifespans (increase) _____will increase_____. How long (our children, live) _____will our children live_____?

↻ UNIT Review

Answer the following questions. If you don't know an answer, go back and review the appropriate section.

1. What is the negative form of will? _____will not / won't_____

2. Correct the verb errors in the sentences below. Then explain why the sentences are incorrect.

   a) In the future, Reena is gonna visit India. _____going to_____

   Reason: _____*Gonna* is not a proper word._____

   b) She will flying with Air Canada. _____will fly_____

   Reason: _____After *will*, use the base form of the verb._____

   c) Do she will travel alone? _____Will she travel_____

   Reason: _____Never add *do* to future tense questions containing *will*._____

   d) When I will have enough money, I will buy a car. _____When I have_____

   Reason: _____Use the simple present in time clauses._____

3. Write the question and negative forms of the following sentences.

    a) Liz will help us.

       Question: _Will Liz help us?_

       Negative: _Liz won't help us._

    b) They are going to buy a solar car.

       Question: _Are they going to buy a solar car?_

       Negative: _They aren't going to buy a solar car._

    c) He is going to move.

       Question: _Is he going to move?_

       Negative: _He isn't going to move._

Need more practice?
Visit the Companion Website and try additional exercises.

Final Review

You can use the Final Review as a test. There are twenty answers in Part A and five in Part B. You can also find additional practice exercises and testing material on the Companion Website.

PART A

Write the verb shown in the correct tense—present, past, or future—in the spaces provided. Use *will* for future tense verbs.

    EXAMPLE: In the future, Jordan (meet) _will meet_ a beautiful woman.

1. Humans (think, often) _____ often think _____ about emotional events from their past. (you, remember) _____ Do you remember _____ your first romance? Many songs are about the strength of that first emotional bond. For example, in 2003, Sheryl Crow (sing) _____ sang _____ "The First Cut Is the Deepest."

2. Last summer, Jordan Reed's girlfriend (leave) _____ left _____ him. Chantal (be) _____ was _____ Jordan's first love. She (provide, not) _____ didn't provide _____ a clear reason for her decision. She told him that they (be, not) _____ weren't _____ compatible.

3. Jordan (feel) _____ felt _____ very sad after they broke up. Nowadays, he (have, not) _____ doesn't have _____ a girlfriend. He (be, not) _____ isn't _____ ready to meet someone else.

4. Canadian scientists are working on a drug that will soften memories of traumatic events. The drug will make negative memories much less intense. In the future, perhaps people (take) _____ will take _____ a pill as soon as they (have) _____ have _____ an intense and difficult experience. They (forget) _____ will forget _____ emotional pain. How much money (the pill, cost) _____ will the pill cost _____?
(be, it) _____ Will it be _____ effective?

5. Jordan says, "Maybe in the future, I (feel) _____ will feel _____ better when I (fall) _____ fall _____ in love with someone else. But I (forget, never) _____ will never forget _____ Chantal." Jordan (take, not) _____ won't take _____ any memory-erasing pills in the future. He says, "In the future, I (try) _____ will try _____ to cherish every moment, both good and bad."

PART B

Underline and correct five errors in future tense forms.

won't
EXAMPLE: Dr. Rahim <u>wont</u> read my palm.

~~will~~
What will our planet <u>will</u> look like in ten years? According to experts, the

won't
population will explode. Some countries <u>wont</u> have enough food and land

rise
for their populations. When sea levels <u>will rise</u>, probably coastal areas will

going to
erode. Perhaps some people are <u>gonna</u> live in outer space. Maybe space

are
shuttles <u>is</u> going to transport people to space colonies.

Are we going to live in outer space one day?

Future Plans

Work with a partner and tell each other about your future plans. Explain at least three things that you will do and at least three things that you won't do after you finish college. Then write a short paragraph describing your partner's future plans.

UNIT 5

The Present Perfect Tense

Additional practice exercises can be found on the Companion Website.

Use the Preview activity to introduce the unit. Then students can complete the unit in class or for homework.

Preview

WHAT IS THE PRESENT PERFECT TENSE?

Use the **present perfect** tense to show that an action began in the past and continues to the present time. (Use it with *since* and *for*.) You can also use this tense to show that past actions occurred at unknown past times.

He **has been** a student at this college since September.

We **have had** three assignments.

MY EXPERIENCES

PART A

Write three sentences about interesting or unusual things that you have done in your life. Use the present perfect tense (*have* + past participle) in your sentences.

EXAMPLE: I have been to Costa Rica.

1. _____

2. _____

3. _____

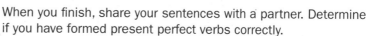

PART B

Now write three sentences about things that you have never done.

EXAMPLE: I have never eaten snake meat.

4. _____
_____

5. _____
_____

6. _____
_____

When you finish, share your sentences with a partner. Determine if you have formed present perfect verbs correctly.

Present Perfect: Forms and Usage

In the **present perfect** tense, you must use the auxiliary *have* or *has* and the past participle.

Alicia **has** <u>lived</u> in Mexico City since 1977.

We **have** <u>met</u> her several times.

Use the present perfect in two different ways:

1. The **present perfect** indicates that an action began in the past and continues to the present time.

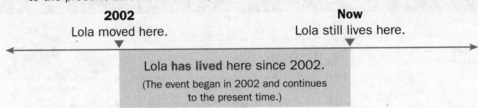

Keywords: never, ever, not yet, so far, up to now, since 2005, for five years ...

2. The **present perfect** indicates that one or more completed past actions occurred at unspecified time(s) in the past.

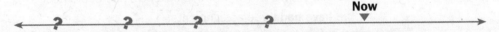

Lola **has visited** Greece many times.

(The visits occurred at unspecified times in the past.)

Keywords: once, twice, several times, many times (before now), lately, recently ...

PAST PARTICIPLES

The **past tense** and the **past participle** of regular verbs are the same. However, they may differ when the verb is irregular. For a list of irregular past participles, see Appendix 3 on page 153.

	BASE FORM	PAST TENSE	PAST PARTICIPLE
Regular	talk carry	talked carried	**talked** **carried**
Irregular	go begin	went began	**gone** **begun**

QUESTION FORM

Place the auxiliary (*have* or *has*) before the subject.

She has worked since 9 a.m.   **Has** she worked since 9 a.m.?

They have been here for hours.   **Have** they been here for hours?

NEGATIVE FORM

Put *not* between the auxiliary and the verb.

They have **not** left yet.   She has **not** finished.

THE PRESENT PERFECT PROGRESSIVE TENSE

The **present perfect progressive** indicates that an action has been in progress from a past time up to the present moment. This tense emphasizes the *duration* of the uninterrupted activity.

Form: have been + <u>verb</u> + *–ing*
            has

    Madhuri **has been talking** for twenty minutes. When will she stop talking?

With some verbs (e.g., *live, work, teach, study*), the **present perfect** and the **present perfect progressive** forms have essentially the same meaning. Compare the following sentences:

Present perfect: Madhuri **has worked** full-time since 2006.

Present perfect progressive: Madhuri **has been working** full-time since 2006.

Practice

EXERCISE 1 RECOGNIZING PAST PARTICIPLE ERRORS

In the following selection, the past participles are underlined. Find and correct ten past participle errors. Write *C* above the correct past participles.

             met
EXAMPLE: We have <u>meeted</u> many times to discuss the problem.

1. Throughout history, people have <u>did</u> many things in the pursuit
     [*done*]

    of pleasure. Archeologists have <u>finded</u> beer jugs from the Stone
     [*found*]

    Age. They have <u>examined</u> ancient honey-fermentation vessels.
     [*C*]

    Since the beginning of human existence, people have also <u>have</u>
     [*had*]

    a love affair with sports. Over the centuries, Homer and others

    have <u>wrote</u> about public games and celebrations.
     [*written*]

2. These days, a surprising new sport has <u>became</u> popular. Since 1997, people
     [*become*]

    of all ages have <u>read</u> the *Harry Potter* books. In the books, Harry and his friends
     [*C*]

    play quidditch, a fictional sport. Over the years, audiences have <u>saw</u> the sport
     [*seen*]

    in *Harry Potter* movies. With the help of special effects, young players have <u>fly</u>
     [*flown*]

    on broomsticks to hit "quaffle" balls and to catch the "snitch," a tiny golden

    ball with wings. Harry Potter has <u>catched</u> the snitch many times.   →
     [*caught*]

3. Since at least 2003, some enterprising *Harry Potter* fans have did [done] a human version of quidditch. Basically, J. K. Rowling has teached [taught] people to play a new and unusual sport.

Exercises 2 to 4 focus on "the past action continues to the present time." To practise, ask students the following types of questions: 1) Who has a car? When did you buy the car? How long have you owned your car? 2) Who is your best friend? When did you meet him/her? How long have you known your best friend?

SINCE, FOR, AND AGO

Use the **present perfect** when a past action continues to the present time. This use of the present perfect generally occurs with the prepositions *for* and *since*.

Present Perfect

Since refers to a specific past time when the action began.

Nicole **has lived** in Calgary **since** 2008. (She is still living there.)

For refers to the amount of time that the action has lasted.

She **has worked** at IBM **for** three years. (She still works there.)

Past

Ago refers to a time in the past when the completed action occurred. Use *ago* with the simple past tense only.

Nicole **married** Sean six years **ago**.

EXERCISE 2 USING *SINCE*, *FOR*, AND *AGO*

Read the following paragraphs and underline eight examples of the present perfect tense. Write *since*, *for*, or *ago* in the spaces provided.

EXAMPLE: He <u>has wanted</u> to be an inventor <u>since</u> he was a little kid.

1. Three years ___ago___, my friend Guy decided that he wanted to be an inventor. ___For___ most of his life, he <u>has tried</u> to develop funny products. ___Since___ he graduated from high school, he <u>has created</u> several novelty items. Two years ___ago___, he developed a "laughing ball." The ball laughs when someone kicks it. ___Since___ then, he <u>has sold</u> many of these balls.

2. Many years ___ago___, Guy was a salesman, but he wasn't happy. ___Since___ he began his new career, he <u>has felt</u> more passionate about his life. Guy <u>has been</u> an inventor ___for___ the last three years. He says, "___Since___ I began, I <u>have not become</u> rich, but I <u>have felt</u> happy. ___For___ the last few years, I <u>have had</u> a great life."

QUESTIONS, NEGATIVES, AND INTERRUPTING WORDS

In **questions**, place the auxiliary *have* or *has* before the subject. In **negative sentences**, place *not* after the auxiliary.

Becky **has been** here since noon.

Has she **been** here since noon? She **has not been** here since noon.

When you add an **interrupting** word such as *also*, *ever*, or *never* to a sentence, place it between the auxiliary and the verb. In questions, place the interrupting word after the subject.

I have **never** been to Brazil. Have you **ever** been there?

TIP

When the Main Verb Is *Have*

Even when the main verb is *have*, you must still use the auxiliary *have* or *has*. Then add the past participle *had*.

My sister **has had** some problems recently.

We **have had** many arguments.

EXERCISE 3 AFFIRMATIVE, NEGATIVE, AND QUESTION FORMS

Fill in the blanks with the present perfect form of the verb.

EXAMPLE: Our lives (change) <u>have changed</u> a lot since the 1990s.

1. How (technology, change) <u>has technology changed</u> our lives? The home computer (have) <u>has had</u> a big effect on the way people live. Most people (stop, not) <u>have not stopped</u> going to a workplace. However, some workers (be) <u>have been</u> able to perform their duties at home. In fact, since 1998, the home office (become) <u>has become</u> the main workplace for millions of North Americans. (you, work, ever) <u>Have you ever worked</u> from home?

2. The home computer (modify, also) <u>has also modified</u> the way that people socialize. How (it, do) <u>has it done</u> that? Online dating sites (help) <u>have helped</u> many people find life partners. Most of those people (try) <u>have tried</u> traditional dating, but they (have, not) <u>have not had</u> success. So online dating (provide) <u>has provided</u> such people with an alternative way to meet potential partners.

TIP

Looking at Keywords

Use keywords to help you decide which tense to use. Be careful: when the past time is stated and other sentences give details about that past time, use the past tense.

I **have been** a traveller **since** I graduated from college. Four years **ago**, I **went** to Greece. I **stayed** at a small youth hostel in Athens, and I **visited** the Acropolis. I **bought** fruit from a local market.

EXERCISE 4 SIMPLE PAST AND PRESENT PERFECT

Fill in the blanks with the simple past tense or the present perfect tense. Underline any keywords that help you decide which tense to use.

EXAMPLE: Many people (use) <u>have used</u> Wikipedia for their research <u>since 2000</u>.

1. In 2000, Nupedia, an online encyclopedia, (hit) _____hit_____ _____ the Web. <u>At that time</u>, only experts (write) _____wrote_____ the entries, and each new entry (take) _____took_____ a long time to be peer reviewed.

2. Then, <u>in late 2000</u>, philosopher Lawrence Sanger (have) _____had_____ a brilliant idea. He (propose) _____proposed_____ another encyclopedia site that anyone could contribute to. <u>Since 2001</u>, Wikipedia (be) _____has been_____ one of the Web's most popular sites.

3. <u>During its first year</u>, Wikipedia contributors (write) _____wrote_____ more than twenty thousand articles in eighteen languages. The site (grow) _____has grown_____ very quickly <u>since then</u>. <u>In recent years</u>, more and more people (make) _____have made_____ the website their primary research tool.

4. <u>For many years</u>, many critics (complain) _____have complained_____ about the site. <u>Since the website started</u>, volunteer editors (try) _____have tried_____ to stop people from posting false information. Another complaint is about the types of articles. <u>Since 2001</u>, many authors (deal) _____have dealt_____ with their favourite topics. Thus, there are more entries about *Star Wars* than about World War II.

© ERPI • REPRODUCTION PROHIBITED

5. In 2002, Wikipedia co-founder Jimmy Wales (choose) _____chose_____ to refuse any advertising on the website. Since then, the website (build) _____has built_____ up a loyal community of volunteer editors. Since its debut, ordinary citizens (contribute) _____have contributed_____ more than twenty million articles to Wikipedia.

To practise the unspecified past usage of the present perfect tense, ask students the following questions: How many cities have you visited? When did you visit them? How many times have you been out of the country? How many times have you seen a particular movie? (Etc.)

PAST ACTIONS OCCURRING AT UNSPECIFIED PAST TIMES

Use the **present perfect** tense when one or more completed actions occurred at unspecified past times.

I **have been** to Mexico. Nicholas **has visited** ten countries.
(The past times are not specified.)

EXERCISE 5 SIMPLE PAST AND PRESENT PERFECT

Fill in the blanks with the simple past or present perfect form of the verb.

EXAMPLE: Sherry (do) _has done_ many dangerous stunts.

1. Quidditch is a game in *Harry Potter* novels. Some colleges (build) ___have built___ _____ quidditch fields, which have three hoops on each end. Students at McGill University (create) _____created_____ a quidditch field in 2007.

2. Young people in many countries (form) _____have formed_____ _____ quidditch teams. For example, there (be) _____have been_____ quidditch matches in Australia, England, Canada, and the US. In 2010, athletes in Argentina (make) _____made_____ _____ some quidditch teams. There are more than four hundred quidditch teams around the world.

3. In the *Harry Potter* movies, players use a broom, and they attempt to put a "quaffle"—or red ball—through a hoop. Over the years, McGill player Jason Ray (buy) _____has bought_____ about eight straw brooms. Last weekend, he (buy) _____bought_____ _____ another straw broom. He often breaks his brooms during matches.

➜

4. Since 2007, players (go) _____ *have gone* _____ to the Quidditch

World Cup. Carrie Volstok (be) _____ *has been* _____ to five World

Cups. In 2011, she (go) _____ *went* _____ to the Quidditch

World Cup in New York state. I (see, never) _____ *have never seen* _____

a quidditch match. (you, watch, ever) _____ *Have you ever watched* _____ a game

of quidditch?

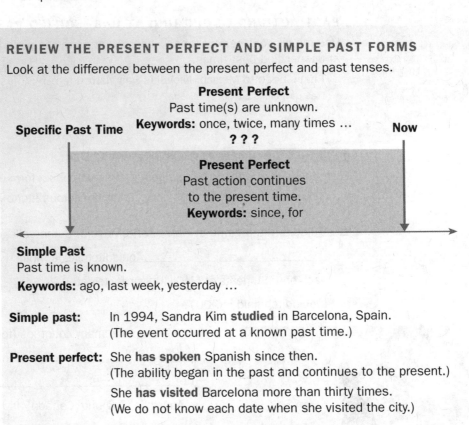

REVIEW THE PRESENT PERFECT AND SIMPLE PAST FORMS

Look at the difference between the present perfect and past tenses.

Present Perfect
Past time(s) are unknown.
Keywords: once, twice, many times …
? ? ?

Specific Past Time

Now

Present Perfect
Past action continues
to the present time.
Keywords: since, for

Simple Past
Past time is known.
Keywords: ago, last week, yesterday …

Simple past: In 1994, Sandra Kim **studied** in Barcelona, Spain.
(The event occurred at a known past time.)

Present perfect: She **has spoken** Spanish since then.
(The ability began in the past and continues to the present.)

She **has visited** Barcelona more than thirty times.
(We do not know each date when she visited the city.)

TIP

Present Perfect or Past?

Use the **past** tense when referring to someone who is no longer living. Use the
present perfect tense only when the action has a relationship to someone or
something that still exists.

wrote
John Lennon ~~has written~~ many songs.
(The past tense is necessary because John Lennon is no longer alive.)

Do not use the present perfect tense when the past time is known.

visited
Two years ago, Elaine ~~has visited~~ Paris.

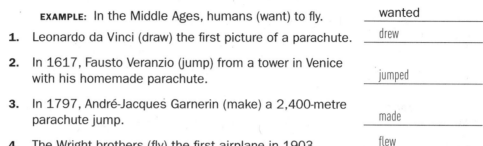

EXERCISE 6 SIMPLE PAST AND PRESENT PERFECT

Fill in the blanks using either the simple past or present tense of the verb indicated.

PART A SIMPLE PAST: THE ACTION FINISHED AT A SPECIFIC PAST TIME.

EXAMPLE: In the Middle Ages, humans (want) to fly. _wanted_

1. Leonardo da Vinci (draw) the first picture of a parachute. _drew_

2. In 1617, Fausto Veranzio (jump) from a tower in Venice with his homemade parachute. _jumped_

3. In 1797, André-Jacques Garnerin (make) a 2,400-metre parachute jump. _made_

4. The Wright brothers (fly) the first airplane in 1903. _flew_

PART B PRESENT PERFECT: THE ACTION BEGAN IN THE PAST AND CONTINUES TO THE PRESENT.

EXAMPLE: Since humans first saw birds, they (want) to fly. _have wanted_

5. Since 1929, commercial airlines (cross) the ocean. _have crossed_

6. For more than one hundred years, people (fly). _have flown_

7. For six years, Niles (own) a small airplane. _has owned_

8. Niles (train) pilots since 2009. _has trained_

PART C PRESENT PERFECT: THE ACTION(S) OCCURRED AT UNSPECIFIED PAST TIMES.

EXAMPLE: I (read) many books about skydiving. _have read_

9. Rianna Roy (do) hundreds of dangerous stunts. _has done_

10. Base jumping is dangerous and illegal. However, Roy and her partner (jump) off buildings twelve times. _have jumped_

11. They (take) several skydiving classes. _have taken_

12. Roy (break) five bones. _has broken_

Ask students to brainstorm questions beginning with these question words.

QUESTION WORDS

Have you ever … ?

Use *have you ever* to determine if something happened at an indefinite past time.

Use *never* to specify that something has not occurred in a person's life.

Have you **ever** been to Brazil? No, I have **never** been there.

How long … ?

Use *how long* to determine the period of time that an action has lasted.

How long has Ms. Malone been the mayor?

How many times … ?

Use *how many times* to ask about the repetition of an activity.

How many times have you been to Kenya?

TIP

Yet

Generally, use the present perfect with *yet*.

Has Amy left yet?

No, she **hasn't** left yet.

EXERCISE 7 INFORMATION QUESTIONS

Turn the following sentences into questions. The answer to each question is in bold.

EXAMPLE: No, I have never been to Spain.   <u>Have you ever been to Spain?</u>

1. Jay Baruchel has been in **about twenty** movies.

    <u>How many movies has Jay Baruchel been in?</u>

2. **No**, he has never forgotten his Canadian roots.

    <u>Has he ever forgotten his Canadian roots?</u>

3. He has lived in Montreal **for most of his life**.

    <u>How long has he lived in Montreal?</u>

4. **No**, his parents have never acted.

    <u>Have his parents ever acted?</u>

5. He has written **five** scripts.

    <u>How many scripts has he written?</u>

6. **No**, he hasn't directed a movie yet.

    <u>Has he directed a movie yet?</u>

EXERCISE 8 MIXED TENSES

PART A

Underline the correct verb form. The verb may be in the present, past, or present perfect tense.

EXAMPLE: Since 1998, new Internet businesses (appear / appeared / <u>have appeared</u> / has appeared) every day.

1. Spying on employees is not new. In fact, companies (do / did / <u>have done</u>) it for many years. Since the 1930s, bosses (listen / listened / <u>have listened</u>) to private conversations. In the last few years, cyberspying (becomes / became / have become / <u>has become</u>) more and more prevalent.

2. Since 2007, many bosses (buy / bought / <u>have bought</u>) SpectorSoft monitoring software. Business owner Martin Scott (purchase / <u>purchased</u> / has purchased) the software in 2009. Every week, he (spy / <u>spies</u> / spied / has spied) on his employees. In fact, since he opened his business, Scott (reads / read / have read / <u>has read</u>) hundreds of employee emails, and he (sees / saw / have seen / <u>has seen</u>) the Internet search history of many employees.

3. Last year, one of Scott's employees (spends / <u>spent</u> / has spent) many work hours looking at online tabloid gossip. Then, on March 14, the employee (sends / <u>sent</u> / has sent) out three resumés. Scott (fires / <u>fired</u> / have fired / has fired) her that day. Since then, he (never regretted / <u>has never regretted</u> / have never regretted) his decision to buy spy software.

PART B
Underline and correct five verb-tense errors.

                              has worked
    EXAMPLE: Since 2007, my brother <u>worked</u> for an advertising company.

4. SpectorSoft president Doug Fowler explains why spy software is necessary.

                                             sold
   Over the years, employees have <u>selled</u> confidential information to

                                          have caught
   competitors. Also, since 2007, many employers <u>caught</u> staff doing illegal

                                        has spent
   activities. For the last three years, my brother's co-worker <u>spent</u> many

   work hours looking at Facebook instead of working. Since 2010, my brother

             worked   wants
   has <u>work</u> too hard. These days, my brother <u>want</u> his boss to buy spy software.

EXERCISE 9 WHO IS IT?
Write the best answer in the spaces provided.

1. Luc has changed a tire.
   Nicolas has been changing a tire.
   Whose clothes are more likely to be dirty?   Nicolas's

2. Mr. White has been jogging.
   Mr. Green has jogged.
   Who is sweaty now?   Mr. White

3. Kaitlin has lived in Nova Scotia for years.
   Kaitlin has been living in Nova Scotia for years.
   Do these sentences have the same meaning?   Yes

4. Carl has been shovelling the snow.
   Mara has shovelled snow.
   Who has a sore back?   Carl

EXERCISE 10 PRESENT PERFECT PROGRESSIVE
Use the present perfect or the present perfect progressive tense. (To review the present perfect progressive tense, see page 55.)

    EXAMPLE: Claire (study) <u>has been studying</u> since noon. She (take) <u>hasn't taken</u> a break.

Answers may vary.

1. Mr. and Mrs. Lavoie love to spend winters by the beach. They (be) __have been__ _____ to Florida several times. Right now, they are returning home. Mrs. Lavoie (drive) _____has been driving_____ for nine hours and she is very tired. Mr. Lavoie (sleep) _____has been sleeping_____ for three hours. Mrs. Lavoie (ask) _____has asked_____ her husband to drive several times, but he (refused) _____has refused_____ each time.

2. They are at the border crossing. They (have, never) _____have never had_____ a problem crossing the border. However, today a guard pulled them over. They (wait) _____have been waiting_____ for two hours. Border guards (inspect) _____have been inspecting_____ their motorhome since 3 p.m.

↻ UNIT Review

Answer the following questions. If you don't know an answer, go back and review the appropriate section.

1. When do you use the present perfect tense? Give two explanations.
   a) __When an action began in the past and continues to the present time.__
   b) __When an action occurred at an unknown or unspecified past time.__

2. Underline and correct the verb errors in the sentences below. Then explain why the sentences are incorrect.
   a) I <u>live</u> here since 2002. __have lived__
      Reason: __The action began in the past and continues to the present.__
   b) Two weeks ago, we <u>have seen</u> the movie. __saw__
      Reason: __The action was completed in the past. Use the past tense.__
   c) For ten years, we <u>have</u> a dog. We love this dog. __have had__
      Reason: __The action began in the past and continues to the present.__
   d) Mike has <u>broke</u> three world records. __broken__
      Reason: __Use the past participle with the present perfect tense.__

3. Put *since* or *for* in the following spaces.
   EXAMPLE: __since__ Wednesday

   __since__ last May   __for__ a few months
   __for__ twelve hours   __since__ he was a child
   __since__ I graduated   __for__ a long time

 Need more practice? Visit the Companion Website and try additional exercises.

Final Review

You can use the Final Review as a test. There are fifteen answers in Part A and five answers in Part B. You can also find additional practice exercises and testing material on the Companion Website.

PART A

Insert the correct form of the verb in parentheses. Use the simple past or the present perfect tense.

EXAMPLE: (you, see, ever) <u>Have you ever seen</u> a viral YouTube video?

1. The Internet (change) _____ has changed _____ many people's lives over the years. For example, since 2005, YouTube (be) _____ has been _____ _____ extremely popular, and many people (find) _____ have found _____ _____ fame with their videos. But not everyone wants online fame.

You can ask students to complete the final review and then detach this page. In the student books, pages are perforated.

2. On November 3, 2002, fifteen-year-old Ghyslain Raza (make) _____ made _____ _____ a video of himself. In the video, Raza pretended that a golf-ball retriever was a laser sword. The next day, a classmate (find) _____ found _____ the video and passed it around. On April 14, 2003, another student (post) _____ posted _____ the video online. Since then, Raza (have) _____ has had _____ the nickname "Star Wars Kid."

3. Since 2003, millions of people (see) _____ have seen _____ Raza with his imaginary laser. The video (receive) _____ has received _____ _____ more than 900 million views! Hundreds of people (make) _____ have made _____ tribute videos to the Star Wars Kid.

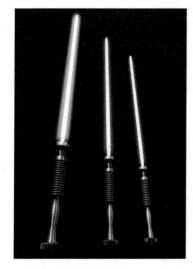

4. Back in 2003, Raza (be) _____ was _____ not happy with his sudden fame. For the next two years, he (feel) _____ felt _____ _____ sad and humiliated. In July 2003, Raza's family (launch) _____ launched _____ a lawsuit against the students who posted the video.

5. Since 2008, Ghyslain Raza (move) _____ has moved _____ _____ past his Star Wars Kid label. In 2009, he (become) _____ became _____ a law student at McGill University. He is now very happy with his life.

PART B

Underline and correct the errors involving verb tense. Write *C* beside any sentences that are correct.

have put
6. Since 2005, many companies put advertisements on YouTube.

made
7. In 2006, a Toronto advertising company has made an interesting ad for Dove.

8. On October 6, 2006, viewers saw the transformation of an ordinary woman into an amazing beauty. C

9. For more than one hundred years, photographers have
modified
modify photos.

seen
10. Have you ever saw the Dove ad?

SPEAKING AND WRITING

Students can do the writing exercise on a separate sheet of paper. Once students have finished, ask them to exchange their writing and peer edit for the correct use of verbs.

Questions

Work with a partner. Write ten questions for one of the following people. Use a variety of verb tenses. (Write at least three questions that include the present perfect tense.)

Choose one:

- A soldier who is fighting in a war
- A fashion model
- A billionaire

EXAMPLE: *(to billionaire)* Have you ever stolen money from someone?

© ERPI • REPRODUCTION PROHIBITED

Pronouns

Preview

Use the Preview activity to introduce pronouns. Students can then complete the unit in class or for homework.

WHAT ARE PRONOUNS?

Pronouns are words that replace nouns, other pronouns, and phrases. Use pronouns to avoid repeating nouns.

He

Farhad has an unusual job. ~~Farhad~~ designs sports stadiums.

PRONOUN CHART

Work with a partner and fill in the missing pronouns.

	SUBJECT PRONOUN	OBJECT PRONOUN	POSSESSIVE ADJECTIVE*	POSSESSIVE PRONOUN	REFLEXIVE PRONOUN
Example	**She** is busy.	A doctor saw **him** yesterday.	Kelly drives **her** car to work.	That house is **ours**.	He went to Spain by **himself**.
Singular	I	me	my	mine	myself
	you	you	your	yours	yourself
	he	him	his	his	himself
	she	her	her	hers	herself
	it	it	its	—	itself
Plural	we	us	our	ours	ourselves
	you	you	your	yours	yourselves
	they	them	their	theirs	themselves

* Technically, possessive adjectives are not pronouns, but they are similar to pronouns, so they are included in this unit.

Pronouns: Forms and Usage

SUBJECT PRONOUNS AND OBJECT PRONOUNS

A **subject pronoun** performs the action and is usually followed by a verb. An **object pronoun** replaces an object and is usually found after a verb or preposition.

subject   object

She   **them**

Officer Mel Wang arrested the bank robbers.

Sentences may have more than one subject or object.

subject   object   object

He   **them**   **it**

Stephen King talked to students about his latest novel.

POSSESSIVE ADJECTIVES AND POSSESSIVE PRONOUNS

Possessive adjectives describe a noun and appear before the noun that they describe. **Possessive pronouns** replace the possessive adjective and noun.

possessive adjective   possessive pronoun

Lola and Rick lost **their** passports.   Did you lose **yours**?

REFLEXIVE PRONOUNS

Use **reflexive pronouns** when the subject doing the action and the object receiving the action are the same person or thing.

The small boy dressed **himself**.

Practice

IS IT A SUBJECT OR AN OBJECT?

When a pronoun is paired with another noun, the correct pronoun type isn't always obvious. A simple way to determine the correct pronoun is to say the sentence with just one pronoun.

The video store hired Jason and (**I** or **me**).

Possible choices: The video store hired I. / The video store hired me.
Answer: The video store hired Jason and **me**.

EXERCISE 1 SUBJECT PRONOUNS AND OBJECT PRONOUNS

PART A

Replace the underlined words with subject pronouns or object pronouns.

It

EXAMPLE: I read a great article the other day. The article was fascinating.

1. Many people feel a lot of pleasure when they look at art. Steve Wynn, a

   renowned casino developer, owns a 1932 Picasso portrait titled "Le Rêve."

   The Picasso portrait _It_ is worth more than $100 million. Wynn invited his friends

   to see the Picasso portrait _it_. Wynn's friends _They_ visited Wynn _him_ at his Las Vegas office.

2. Wynn stood in front of his friends and bragged,

   "Someone is going to pay $139 million for the painting _it_."

   While Wynn _he_ was showing the painting to his friends _them_, he

   gestured with his arms. Wynn _He_ accidentally put his elbow

   through the painting.

3. Stunned, everyone looked at the painting and at Wynn _him_.

   Wynn looked at one of the guests, the writer Nora Ephron.

   Wynn _He_ said to Nora _her_, "Don't write about this on your blog!"

   Later, when Nora wrote about the accident _it_ on her blog,

   Steve Wynn _he_ and Nora stopped speaking.

PART B

Underline the correct pronoun in parentheses.

    EXAMPLE: My mother and (<u>I</u> / me) often discuss art.

4. My mother told my brother and (I / <u>me</u>) the Steve Wynn story. My mother said
   that if (her / <u>she</u>) had a Picasso, she would not show it to my brother and
   (I / <u>me</u>). My brother and (<u>I</u> / me) would never get near it. (<u>We</u> / Us) laughed
   because (<u>she</u> / her) will never own a Picasso. But if my brother and (<u>I</u> / me)
   had a lot of money, maybe we would buy one for (she / <u>her</u>). Then she would
   thank my brother and (I / <u>me</u>).

TIP

Avoid Double Subjects

Do not repeat the subject with the pronoun form. (A subject pronoun *replaces* the
subject.)

    Mr. Ross ~~he~~ is friendly.

EXERCISE 2 IDENTIFY DOUBLE SUBJECTS

Delete five double subjects in the paragraphs below.

> **EXAMPLE:** My brother and sister ~~they~~ are not superstitious.

1. Montreal has the largest subterranean city in the world. In 1962, construction ~~it~~ began under Place Ville-Marie. Today, the underground complex ~~it~~ stretches for 32 kilometres. There are many places where shoppers ~~they~~ can enter the underground city. It has more than two hundred entrances. Commuters ~~they~~ can take the subway because there are ten subway stations in the tunnels. Montreal ~~it~~ has harsh winters, so it is convenient that shoppers can stay indoors.

CHOOSING *HIS*, *HER*, OR *ITS*

To choose the correct **possessive adjective**, think about the possessor, not the object that is possessed.

If something belongs to a female, use ***her***.	If something belongs to a male, use ***his***.	If something belongs to or is part of an object, use ***its***.

her brother	**his** car	**its** muffler
her father	**his** mother	**its** wheels
her house	**his** daughter	**its** seat

EXERCISE 3 POSSESSIVE FORMS

Underline the correct possessive pronoun or possessive adjective.

> **EXAMPLE:** He bought (<u>his</u> / her) trampoline fifteen years ago.

1. According to psychologists, play is not simply an indulgence. Games are crucial for (<u>our</u> / ours) health and happiness. For example, when I was a child, (<u>our</u> / ours) neighbours had a trampoline. Mr. Weiss said, "I know that this trampoline is (our / <u>ours</u>), but you can use it any time. Act like it is (your / <u>yours</u>), too."

TIP

Possessive Forms

Possessive adjectives describe a noun and appear before the noun that they describe, as in *her* car and *our* house. **Possessive pronouns** replace the possessive adjective and noun, as in *the car is* **hers** and *that house is* **ours**.

2. At first, I was very shy to use (their / theirs) trampoline. I said, "It is not (my / mine)! I don't want to enter (your / yours) yard without permission." Eventually, (my / mine) brother and I got over (our / ours) shyness. We played in (our / ours) yard, but we also played in (their / theirs).

3. I am now an adult, and I still see the value of play. Sometimes my girlfriend and I invite (our / ours) friends over, and we play darts and board games. We can use (our / ours) games or (their / theirs). We aren't competitive. Sometimes we play for quarters. My brother remembers to bring his spare change, but (his / her) girlfriend usually forgets to bring (her / hers).

COMMONLY CONFUSED WORDS

Do not confuse the following pronouns with similar-sounding words.

His is a possessive adjective or pronoun.   Jeff works with **his** brother.
Is is a form of the verb *be*.   He **is** a hard worker.
He's means "He is."   **He's** busy today.

Its is a possessive adjective.   The office has **its** annual party in May.
It's is the contraction of *it is*.   **It's** a very nice party.

Your is a possessive adjective.   **Your** dog is cute.
You're is the contraction of *you are*.   **You're** a great friend.

Their is a possessive adjective.   **Their** car is old.
They're is the contraction of *they are*.   **They're** going to move.
There indicates that something exists   **There** are many police officers
or where it is.   on the street over **there**.

EXERCISE 4 MIXED PRONOUNS AND POSSESSIVE ADJECTIVES

Underline the correct word in parentheses. If no pronoun is required, underline X.

1. Sports are important for health and happiness. With sports, (we / us / X) learn to correct (our / ours) mistakes and accept failure. Football has (it's / its) faults, but generally (it's / its) an exciting sport.

2. On November 14, 2004, during a playoff game, the Saskatchewan Roughriders (they / it / X) had a chance to win. The team had (its / her / his) best players on the field. During overtime, Paul McCallum prepared to score the winning field goal. The ball (it / he / she / X) was on the eighteen-yard line, so McCallum could easily kick (her / him / it) and score three points. He looked at his fans, and he

→

wanted to make (they / their / <u>them</u>) happy. "(Their / <u>They're</u> / There) going to cheer," he thought. "(<u>It's</u> / Its) an easy goal." McCallum kicked the ball, but (<u>his</u> / her) aim was off, and the ball missed the goalposts. (<u>His</u> / Her / It's) team lost the game.

3. My sister and (<u>I</u> / me) didn't see the game, but many people in (ours / <u>our</u>) family saw it. My uncle told my sister and (I / <u>me</u>) about the Roughriders. "(<u>You're</u> / Your) lucky you didn't see (there / <u>their</u> / they're) faces when they lost," he said. After the loss, the fans were furious with McCallum. Someone put manure on (<u>his</u> / its / it's) lawn, and others made death threats against (he / her / <u>him</u>). I think (<u>it's</u> / its / X) ridiculous that fans would treat one of (<u>their</u> / theirs / there) own players so badly. (<u>You're</u> / your) a true fan if you love (you're / <u>your</u>) favourite players even when they have a bad day.

REFLEXIVE PRONOUNS

Use **reflexive pronouns** when the subject doing the action and the object receiving the action are the same person or thing. You cannot say, "She dressed himself" because *himself* doesn't correspond to the female subject *she*. Note that the expression "by oneself" means "alone."

She can drive home **by herself**.

Remember that *you* has both singular and plural reflexive pronouns.

yourself (one person: you)

yourselves (more than one person: you and others)

TIP

Reflexive Pronoun Errors

Do not use *hisself* or *theirselves*. These are incorrect ways to say *himself* and *themselves*.

                   themselves   **himself**
Our friends helped ~~theirselves~~ to the food. Gary ate by ~~hisself~~.

EXERCISE 5 **REFLEXIVE PRONOUNS**

Write the correct reflexive pronouns in the blanks.

    EXAMPLE: I often talk to <u>myself</u>.

1. My brothers and I went cross-country skiing by _____ourselves_____.

   When we were in a remote area, I was behind the others. I fell and hurt
   _____myself_____. My brothers continued on by _____themselves_____.

   I started yelling, but nobody heard me.

2. Suddenly, I heard a noise. A strange woman was hiking by _____herself_____.
She asked, "What are you doing here by _____yourself_____?" In her backpack
she had a first-aid kit. She expertly bound up my ankle. She carried my skis, and
I supported _____myself_____ using my ski poles.

3. Later, I met my brothers at the parking lot. I was angry and said to them, "You
are selfish! You two only care about _____yourselves_____." My brothers felt
ashamed of _____themselves_____ because they had left me alone in the woods.

EXERCISE 6 MIXED PRONOUNS AND POSSESSIVE ADJECTIVES
Fill in the blanks with a pronoun or a possessive adjective.

1. In the early 1930s, Charles Darrow was an unemployed salesman. At the
time, nobody would hire _____him_____, so he could not support
_____his_____ family. One day, he decided to work on a board game
about buying and selling property. Then he went to a department store by
_____himself_____. He sold five thousand games of Monopoly. People
bought the game and played with _____their_____ friends.

2. In 1935, Parker Brothers bought Darrow's game and then paid royalties to
_____him_____. Soon, Darrow became rich. Parker Brothers still credits
_____him_____ as the sole inventor of Monopoly. However, there was a
problem. Some people speculate that he simply copied the rules of a popular
land-renting game, and _____he_____ changed some of the details.

3. Thirty years earlier, Miss Lizzie Magie got a patent for _____her_____
board game. Magie created The Landlord's Game by _____herself_____.
The idea was _____hers_____. When she tried to sell the game to Parker
Brothers, the game company refused to buy _____it_____. Parker
Brothers said, "You have a good idea, but _____your_____ game is
too complicated. Nobody will buy _____it_____."

4. Magie replied, "I don't agree. I have my
opinion and you have _____yours_____."
She was angry with _____them_____,
but there was nothing that she could do. After
Monopoly became successful, Parker Brothers
employees looked for Magie and paid
_____her_____ $500.

5. My wife and I often play Monopoly with _____ our _____ neighbours. We

play in our house or _____ theirs _____ . We don't use the online version.

_____ Our _____ preference is for the classic board game. Do you ever

play board games with _____ your _____ friends?

PRONOUN CONSISTENCY

A paragraph or essay should have a consistent point of view in the general sections. Avoid making illogical or unnecessary pronoun shifts.

Sometimes a shift occurs within a sentence. Make sure that the pronoun agrees with the antecedent.

       ⟶ **their**

The <u>students</u> should finish ~~her~~ work.

Pronoun shifts can also occur within a paragraph.

          ⟶ **they**

<u>People</u> started to riot. It was so crowded that ~~you~~ couldn't move.

Consistency with Indefinite Pronouns

Indefinite pronouns are words such as *nothing*, *anybody*, and *something*. They are singular, so you should use a singular pronoun to refer to them. If you don't know the gender of the person, you can use *his or her*.

      his or her

<u>Everybody</u> carried ~~their~~ lunch.

If the sentence is awkward, simply change the subject to the plural form.

Incorrect: Everybody packed **their** bags.

Solution: Everybody packed **his or her** bags.

Better solution: The students packed **their** bags.

EXERCISE 7 **IDENTIFY ERRORS**

Answers will vary.

Underline and correct one pronoun or word-choice error in each sentence.

             your

  EXAMPLE: You should enjoy life with ~~you're~~ friends.

                their

1. In the pursuit of pleasure, many people take <u>theirs</u> children to Disneyland.

2. The Florida and California Disney theme parks are very successful, so the

            its

Disney Company decided to bring <u>it's</u> parks to other countries.

                   his or her *or* people lined up ...

3. In 1983, Tokyo Disneyland opened, and everyone lined up to buy <u>their</u> tickets.

4. On the first day, thousands of people entered the park. It was so crowded that

  they

<u>you</u> couldn't walk easily.

himself or herself or people enjoyed …

5. It's certain that everyone enjoyed <u>themselves</u>.

their

6. Then Disney executives decided to open a park in France, but <u>they're</u> decision led to some problems.

their

7. Many French intellectuals said that <u>there</u> culture was being attacked by Americans.

themselves

8. Some of the employees helped <u>theirselves</u> to part of the park's receipts.

his

9. A top Disney chairman nearly lost <u>is</u> job when the park lost more than a billion dollars in the first two years of operation.

you're

10. When <u>your</u> in Paris, you may notice that Disney has significantly changed the park to accommodate French interests.

its

11. The park was originally called Euro Disneyland, but in 1995, <u>it's</u> name was changed to Disneyland Paris.

12. When my cousin and I visited Paris, we visited the park. The workers were very

me

friendly to my cousin and <u>I</u>.

In the final Editing Practice and Tense Review unit, beginning on page 144, students can edit a student paragraph and correct shifts in the point of view.

↻ UNIT Review

Answer the following questions. If you don't know an answer, go back and review the appropriate section.

1. Fill in the missing object pronouns below.

a) I _____ me _____ c) he _____ him _____ e) it _____ it _____ g) they _____ them _____

b) you _____ you _____ d) she _____ her _____ f) we _____ us _____

2. Correct the pronoun errors in the following sentences.

a) My sister moved in with <u>his</u> boyfriend.   _____ her _____

b) The boys sometimes help <u>theirselves</u> to food.   _____ themselves _____

c) Adela <u>she</u> is a really hard worker.   _____ remove *she* _____

d) Look at the baby! He can feed <u>hisself</u> now.   _____ himself _____

e) The Johnsons leave <u>there</u> doors unlocked.   _____ their _____

f) We put <u>ours</u> dogs outside.   _____ our _____

Need more practice? Visit the Companion Website and try other pronoun exercises.

© ERPI • REPRODUCTION PROHIBITED

UNIT 6 | **Pronouns** | 75

Final Review

You can use the Final Review as a test. There are twenty answers in Part A and five answers in Part B. You can also find additional practice exercises and testing material on the Companion Website.

PART A

Underline the correct word in parentheses. Note that *X* means "nothing."

   EXAMPLE: They enjoyed (theirselves / <u>themselves</u>) at the event.

1. A "typo" is a mistake that someone makes while (they / <u>he or she</u> / him or her / X) is typing. (Its / <u>It's</u>) a serious problem for many companies.

2. Many years ago, a typo in a computer program caused a space probe to blow up. (<u>It</u> / He / She) caused NASA to lose $80 million. I asked (me / <u>myself</u>) if this story could be true. My father and (<u>I</u> / me) couldn't believe that one added hyphen could cause a catastrophe like that.

3. My mother (she / <u>X</u>) became very curious. She asked my father and (I / <u>me</u>) to tell (<u>her</u> / hers) the story. She did not believe (we / <u>us</u> / ourselves). We have (<u>our</u> / ours) ideas about the truth, and she has (her / <u>hers</u> / X).

4. Mr. Carlos Diaz and (me / <u>I</u>) decided to research other damaging typos. I searched for stories on my computer and Carlos searched on (he's / hers / <u>his</u>). (<u>Our</u> / Ours) research turned up more facts.

5. Software developers for the New York City Department of Transportation made some typos in (<u>their</u> / theirs) accounting software. The errors caused the money spent on transportation to double. When city officials audited (itself / theirselves / <u>themselves</u>), they realized that they had spent $1.4 million extra on transportation. These days, (their / there / <u>they're</u>) much more careful!

6. Programmers should always be sure to check (<u>their</u> / there / they're) spelling. A small error can have big consequences. I always double-check my accounting, so why shouldn't they double-check (their / <u>theirs</u>)? Have you ever made typing errors in (<u>your</u> / you're) life?

PART B

Identify and correct five errors in the underlined words. If the word is correct, write *C*.

EXAMPLE: Some typos have changed <u>ours</u> lives.
our

7. Computer programmers at a lottery company made a serious error.

    Employees mailed out fifty thousand of <u>theirs</u> scratch cards, and all
    their

    of <u>them</u> had a $1000 prize. But only one card was supposed to be
    C

    a winner. The people who bought the scratch cards probably

    couldn't believe <u>there</u> good fortune. The company checked <u>it's</u>
    their *its*

    computers, and then officials <u>they</u> quickly recalled the cards.
    ~~they~~

    Computer programmers should always be sure to check <u>their</u>
    C

    spelling. Otherwise, <u>they</u> have only <u>theirselves</u> to blame when
    C *themselves*

    something goes wrong.

SPEAKING AND WRITING

Students can do the writing exercise on a separate sheet of paper. Once students have finished, ask them to exchange their writing and peer edit for correct pronoun usage.

Describe a Celebrity

Write six sentences describing a popular celebrity. Do not mention the celebrity's name. Then exchange sheets with a partner. Underline all the pronouns on your partner's sheet, and then guess who the celebrity is.

EXAMPLE: <u>She</u> adopted many children.
<u>She</u> travels around the world with <u>her</u> husband.
<u>They</u> both act, and <u>their</u> movies are very popular.
Many of <u>her</u> movies are action films.

_____

_____

_____

_____

_____

_____

_____

_____

_____

_____

Modals

Preview

Use the Preview activity to
introduce modals. Students
can then complete the unit
in class or for homework.

WHAT ARE MODAL AUXILIARIES?

Modal auxiliaries are a special class of words. They indicate functions, attitude,
and mood. Modals have no third-person-singular form.

Compare: Samir **can** speak German.   Samir **should** visit Germany.

ADVICE LETTERS

Work with a partner and read the following e-mails. Discuss what each writer should
do. Then write letters of advice to the writers.

I really want to be a famous actor, but I was not accepted into
my college's theatre program. Should I move to Hollywood,
California, and try to become famous? I don't have much
money, but I am sure I will succeed. What should I do?

Kendra

I'm sixteen years old and I'm
very lonely. I am very shy and
cannot meet people easily.
Recently, I met a nice guy on the
Internet. He's nineteen and he
lives in another city. He wants to
send me a bus ticket to visit him.
Should I go?

Alexandra

Last week, I saw my girlfriend flirting
with another guy. I secretly read her
text messages because I thought that
she was cheating on me. She found
out that I had read her texts, and she
got angry. I think that couples should
have no secrets. Should I have read
her text messages?

Devon

Modal Auxiliaries: Forms and Usage

Modal auxiliaries are a special class of words that indicate things such as ability (*can*) and obligation (*must*). Remember that modals have no third-person-singular form.

COMMON MODAL AUXILIARIES			
FUNCTION	**MODAL**	**EXAMPLE**	**PAST FORM**
ability	**can**	She **can speak** English.	**could speak**
polite request	**may** **would** **could** **can**	**May** I **help** you? (formal) **Would** Raul **like** some tea? **Could** you **pass** the butter? **Can** I **help** you? (informal)	
advice	**should** **ought to**	Steve **should stay** with us. The doctor **ought to see** her.	**should have stayed** **ought to have seen**
obligation	**must** **have to***	Jason **must leave** now. She **has to leave** now.	**had to leave** (past form of both *must* and *have to*)
probability	**must**	The store **must be** open.	**must have been**
possibility	**could** **might** **may**	Dan **could help** you. Mary **might do** the job. Ann **may help** them.	**could have helped** **might have done** **may have helped**
condition	**would**	If I had time, I **would help** her. (expresses a wish)	**would have helped**
desire preference	**would like** **would rather**	I **would like** some coffee. I **would rather be** happy than rich.	**would have liked** **would rather have been**

* Although *have to* is not a modal auxiliary, it is included in this list because it functions like a modal and has the same meaning as *must*. The third-person-singular form is *has to*. For the past, use *had to*, and for the future, use *will have to*.

Note: The modal *shall* is rarely used in North America. In Britain, *shall* can replace *should* when asking a polite question (*Shall I help you?*). *Shall* can also be used instead of *will* to indicate a future action (*I shall phone you tomorrow*).

Practice

EXERCISE 1 ANALYZE MODALS

Answer the following questions. You can refer to the previous chart.

1. One of the modals in the chart is actually a regular verb and requires an –s in the third-person-singular form. Which one is it?

   have to

2. Do the other modals need an –s when the subject is third-person singular?

   _No_

3. Which two modals indicate advice?

   should, ought to

4. Which two modals indicate obligation?

   must, have to

→

5. Which three modals indicate possibility? _____could, might, may____

6. Read the sentences below and then answer the question that follows.

Debra *must rest*. Suvendu *has to rest*.

Both of the verb phrases have the same
past form. What is it? _____had to rest_____

POLITE REQUESTS

May, *would*, *could*, and *can* express different levels of requests, from formal (or
most polite) to informal.

Most polite	**May**	**May** I help you? (Use *may* with the pronouns *I* or *we*.)
↓	**Would**	**Would** you like some coffee?
	Could	**Could** you pass the salt?
Informal	**Can**	**Can** I borrow your eraser? (Use *can* with family and friends. Use more polite forms with strangers and people in positions of authority.)

TIP

Negative Forms of Modals

Look at the negative forms of the following modals. Notice that the negative form
of *can* is one word, *cannot*. You can contract the negative forms of most modals.

should not	could not	would not	**cannot**
↓	↓	↓	↓
shouldn't	couldn't	wouldn't	can't

EXERCISE 2 POLITE REQUESTS

Answers will vary.

Write *may*, *would*, *could*, or *can* in the blanks. Use the affirmative or negative forms.
Sometimes more than one choice is acceptable.

1. Landlord: How _____can / may_____ I help you?

2. Tenant: _____May / Could_____ I see the apartment on Friday?

3. Landlord: No, you _____can't / cannot_____. I'm busy that day. _____Could /Can_____

_____ you come on Saturday?

4. Tenant: Of course. We _____can_____ be there at noon. _____Would_____

_____ we have to provide any financial information?

We are students. _____Could / Would_____ you accept our application

if we don't work full-time?

5. Landlord: O.K., but I do need financial information. _____Could / Can_____ you provide your banking documents? I _____would_____ like to do a credit check.

6. Tenant: Of course. _____Would_____ you like any more information?

EXERCISE 3 MODAL CHOICES

Answer the following questions. Read the questions and the three sentences under each of them, and then write your answers on the lines provided.

1. Who has no choice? _____Mike_____
   a) Mike must buy nails.
   b) Carolyn should buy nails.
   c) Samir could buy nails.

2. Which two sentences have the same meaning? _____b and c_____
   a) Samir can help Mike.
   b) Samir should help Mike.
   c) Samir ought to help Mike.

3. Mike loves his job. What is good advice? _____a_____
   a) He shouldn't find another job.
   b) He must find another job.
   c) He couldn't find another job.

4. Which sentence is most polite? _____b_____
   a) Can I help you?
   b) May I help you?
   c) Should I help you?

5. What is most likely making a hole in the wall? _____A rat_____
   a) It could be a dog.
   b) It may be a mouse.
   c) It has to be a rat.

6. Who has no choice? _____Samir_____
   a) Mike should go home.
   b) Carolyn ought to go home.
   c) Samir has to go home.

7. What is the spice in the soup? _____turmeric_____
   a) It may be paprika.
   b) It might be cumin.
   c) It must be turmeric.

ABILITY AND OBLIGATION

Present and Past Ability

Can indicates a present ability. *Could* indicates a past ability.

Ability: Aldo **can speak** Italian. When he was younger, he **could write** in Italian too.

Note that *could* also means that something is possible.

He **could help** you learn Italian.

Present and Past Obligation

Must and *have to* indicate a present obligation. *Had to* indicates a past obligation.

Present: I **have to leave**. I **must work** tonight.

Past: I **had to work** last night, too.

EXERCISE 4 PRESENT AND PAST MODALS

Write the appropriate modal and verb in the spaces provided. The function of each modal is indicated in parentheses. (Sometimes there is more than one possible answer.)

1. When you see a wild animal in the city, you (*advice*: touch, not) _____should not touch_____ it. You (*possibility*: contract) _____could / may / might contract_____ a dangerous disease. For example, you (*possibility*: get) _____could / may / might get_____ rabies or Lyme disease.

2. In past centuries, city dwellers (*past ability*: avoid, not) _____couldn't avoid_____ _____ contact with animals. People (*past obligation*: share) _____had to share_____ their homes with rats and mice. Many citizens (*past ability*: understand, not) _____couldn't understand_____ that diseases such as the bubonic plague, or "Black Death," were transmitted from animals to humans.

3. These days, there are actions that city officials (*ability*: take) _____can take_____ _____. According to experts, cities (*advice*: create) _____should / ought to create_____ more parks and green space for wildlife. Many scientists (*desire*: like) _____would like_____ a more biodiverse landscape.

4. Though we (*ability*: eliminate, not) _____can't eliminate_____ the dangers involved in contact with animals, we (*ability*: create) _____can create_____ urban environments that are healthier for humans and animals.

TIP

Must Not Versus *Don't Have To*

Both **must** and **have to** indicate that something is necessary. However, the meanings are different in the negative form.

Must not means it is not permitted.

You **must not work** today. You are too sick, and you are contagious.

Don't have to means there is no obligation, but you can do it if you want.

You **don't have to stay** in bed. You can watch TV if you prefer.

EXERCISE 5 *MUST NOT* AND *DON'T HAVE TO*

Ask students to think of things they don't have to do in class. They should also think of things they *must not* do.

Write the negative form of either *must* or *have to* in each of the following sentences.

   must not   *don't have to*   *doesn't have to*

EXAMPLE: Children <u>must not</u> touch the electric fence. It is very dangerous.

1. In hospitals, people _____<u>must not</u>_____ use their cellphones. It is forbidden.

2. In India, you _____<u>must not</u>_____ point your feet at other people. It is considered extremely impolite.

3. In Canada, you _____<u>don't have to</u>_____ use the terms *Sir* or *Madam* when speaking with strangers. However, you can use those terms to show respect.

4. On the highway, you _____<u>must not</u>_____ drive backwards. It is illegal and extremely dangerous.

5. In Mexico, Alicia _____<u>doesn't have to</u>_____ use complete names with friends. Many people have nicknames. For example, her friend "Anastacio" is nicknamed "Tacho."

6. When you cross the border from the United States to Canada, you _____<u>must not</u>_____ _____ bring a gun with you. It is illegal.

THE PAST TENSE OF *SHOULD, COULD,* AND *WOULD*

To form the past tense of **should, could,** * and **would**, add *have* + the past participle.

  Present   Past
  could help   **could have helped**

Before Anik and Richard went to Brazil, they **should have learned** a few words in Portuguese. They **could have communicated** with the locals. They **would have had** a better time.

* *Could* refers to a possibility, not a past ability.

EXERCISE 6 PAST FORMS OF MODALS

Write the past form of each modal verb.

> **EXAMPLE:** Some people watched the fire. They (should, leave) <u>should have left</u> because the fire was dangerous.

1. Builders constructed our town in the middle of the forest near the Rocky Mountains. They (should, put) _____ should have put _____ a fire barrier around the town. Also, they built each house out of wood, but they (could, use) _____ could have used _____ cement instead.

2. Our roof caught fire because the tar shingles were flammable. The builders (could, put) _____ could have put _____ an aluminum roof on our house, but they didn't. Also, we had a gas stove in the kitchen. Maybe we (should, have, not) _____ shouldn't have had _____ a gas stove. It exploded and completely destroyed the house. Our important documents burned in the fire. We (should, put) _____ should have put _____ them in a fireproof safe.

3. When we heard the fire alarm, we (have to, leave) _____ had to leave _____ _____ quickly. We (can, stay, not) _____ could not stay _____ in our house. We drove to a neighbouring town. We (must, stay) _____ had to stay _____ in a hotel for three months. We had no choice.

QUESTION FORMS

In **question forms**, move the modal auxiliary before the subject.

They can dance well.	**Can** they dance well?
She should leave.	**Should** she leave?
He could have helped.	**Could** he have helped?

Have to is a regular verb. You must add an auxiliary (*do, does, did*) to make the question form.

They have to leave.	**Do** they **have to** leave?

EXERCISE 7 QUESTION FORMS

Write questions. The exact answer is in bold.

> **EXAMPLE:** The landlord should meet us **tomorrow**. <u>When should he meet us?</u>

1. Amber and Lucas should move to Montreal **because they both work in the city**.
   Why should they move to Montreal?

2. She has to drive every day **because she lives in a suburb**.
   Why does she have to drive every day?

3. She could drive with **a friend**.

Who could she drive with? _____

4. They must pay for **gas**.

What must they pay for? _____

5. They should **take the subway**.

What should they do? / What should they take? _____

6. She would like **a bigger apartment**.

What would she like? _____

7. They should have saved their money **because Montreal rents are expensive**.

Why should they have saved their money? _____

8. Lucas could have helped **Amber**.

Who could Lucas have helped? _____

USE STANDARD PAST FORMS

Some people say *should of* or *shoulda*. These are non-standard forms and you should avoid using them, especially in written communication. When you use the past forms of *should*, *would*, and *could*, always include *have* + the past participle.

should have

Before he went to Japan, he ~~shoulda~~ learned about Japanese business etiquette.

TIP

Never Write *Gotta*

Often, you'll hear people say *gotta*. However, it isn't a proper word, and it should never be written. Make a habit of using *have to* instead of *got to* or *gotta*.

have to

I ~~gotta~~ finish this report.

EXERCISE 8 IDENTIFY ERRORS

Underline and correct the errors in modal forms below. If a sentence is correct, write *C* beside it.

should have visited
EXAMPLE: Last year, we <u>should visited</u> Vancouver.

have to
1. I <u>gotta</u> tell you about my adventures.

could have visited
2. Last year, I <u>could visited</u> Toronto, but I went to New York instead. ➔

3. Before leaving, I <u>should searched</u> for a reasonably priced hotel. *should have searched*

4. Most hotels were full because of a huge conference. We had to <u>stayed</u> at a hotel near Times Square. *stay*

5. The hotel was dirty and expensive. We <u>should stayed</u> somewhere else. *should have stayed*

6. While we were in New York, I really had to <u>saw</u> the Statue of Liberty. *see*

7. I should have taken more photos of the statue. C

8. We <u>woulda</u> stayed longer, but we ran out of money. *would have*

9. I could <u>of</u> borrowed money from my parents, but I didn't. *have*

10. When my sister goes to New York, she should <u>visits</u> the Statue of Liberty. *visit*

↩ UNIT   Review

Answer the following questions. If you don't know an answer, go back and review the appropriate section.

1. Which modal means "ability"? _____ *can* _____

2. Underline the three modals that express possibility. Circle the modal that expresses advice.

   <u>could</u>   have to   <u>might</u>   <u>may</u>   must   (should)

3. Underline the negative modal form that means "it isn't an obligation."

   must not   <u>don't have to</u>

4. Underline and correct the errors in the following sentences.

   EXAMPLE: He could helps.   _could help_

   a) You <u>shouldn't eating</u> too fast.   _shouldn't eat_

   b) When <u>you can teach</u> me to drive?   _can you teach_

   c) He <u>should of left</u> earlier last night.   _should have left_

5. Write the past forms of the modal verbs.

   EXAMPLE: She **can speak** Hindi.   _could speak_

   a) She **can fix** computers.   _could fix_

   b) He **should see** a doctor.   _should have seen_

   c) We **have to leave**.   _had to leave_

   d) Abby **must go** home.   _had to go_

Need more practice?
Visit the Companion Website and try additional exercises about modals.

You can use the Final Review as a test. There are twenty answers in Part A and five answers in Part B, for a total of twenty points. You can also find additional practice exercises and testing material on the Companion Website.

PART A

Underline the correct answer.

1. (Would / Could / Should) you like to go to Singapore? That place has some of the most stringent anti-littering laws in the world. Citizens (must to be / must be / must been) careful. When people throw litter on the ground, they (could face / could have faced) a very severe punishment. What (would the police do / the police would do)? They (might to force / might forcing / might force) an offender to pay a fine or do community service. So in Singapore, people (must not litter / don't have to litter) because it is illegal.

2. Back in 1968, Singapore's leader launched a "Keep Singapore Clean" campaign. Before that, people (can littered / could litter / could littered) without penalty. You (would not liked / wouldn't have liked / wouldn't had liked) to be in Singapore at that time. It was very dirty and polluted.

3. The government (had to did / had to do / must do) something, so it passed tough laws. For example, in 1992, officials noticed that too many people were spitting gum on the sidewalks, so the government banned chewing gum. That summer, citizens (can't bought / couldn't buy / couldn't bought) gum in stores.

4. Every year, many citizens are fined or arrested for littering. How much (can be the fine / can the fine be / do the fine can be)? The largest fine is $3000 Canadian. In 2008, more than 40,000 people were arrested for littering, and they immediately (had to pay / must paid) their fines. For example, last year, Kevin Yu (had to went / had to go / must go) to Singapore for business. While he was there, he threw a tissue on the ground. He (shouldn't had done / shouldn't have did / shouldn't have done) it. A police officer saw him litter, so Kevin (can't deny / couldn't deny) it. He received a large fine.

5. Often, litterers (must do / must doing / has to do) community service as punishment. Offenders (can clean / have to clean / would clean) up the streets while wearing bright jackets. They have no choice. The idea is to shame the offenders so that they won't do it again. If you travel to Singapore,

what (you should do / <u>should you do</u>)? Don't litter! In fact, citizens in every country (<u>shouldn't litter</u> / shouldn't have littered). Generally, people (<u>can keep</u> / would keep / had to keep) garbage in their pockets until they find a garbage can.

You can ask students to remove this page and hand it in. Pages in the students' books are perforated.

PART B

Write the past forms of the underlined modals and verbs.

	Past Form (e.g., yesterday)
EXAMPLE: Kevin <u>has to leave</u>.	had to leave
6. Kevin Yu <u>shouldn't chew</u> gum.	shouldn't have chewed
7. He <u>could put</u> his gum in the garbage.	could have put
8. He <u>has to pay</u> a fine.	had to pay
9. He <u>can't leave</u> at any time.	couldn't leave
10. I <u>would respect</u> the law.	would have respected

SPEAKING AND WRITING

Students can do the writing exercise on a separate sheet of paper. Once students have finished, ask them to recite the dialogue. Then teams of students could exchange sheets and peer edit for correct use of modals.

Dialogue

Work with a partner. Write a dialogue for each situation. Use some modals and the verb *have to* in your dialogues.

SITUATION A

- Ella Smith was born rich, and she loves to spend money. She has just spent $70,000 on a new Lexus, even though she already has four other cars. Yesterday, she spent $35,000 for a two-month cruise. She will leave next month.
- Mr. Charron is an accountant. His client, Ella Smith, has huge debts and a very large tax bill that she hasn't paid yet. She could face bankruptcy or go to prison if she does not take action and reduce her expenses. Mr. Charron tries to convince Mrs. Smith to cancel her cruise, sell some of her cars, and spend much less.

SITUATION B

- Officer Hudson has just stopped a speeding driver. Nadia was going 80 kph in a 35-kph zone.
- Nadia fears she will lose her licence if she gets another speeding ticket. She offers the officer some money. The officer is tempted to accept the bribe but would like more money.

EXAMPLE: Ella Smith: I want to go on a cruise.
Mr. Charron: You shouldn't do that.
Ella Smith: But I'm really tired. I must take a break. I have already paid for the cruise.
Etc.

UNIT 8 — Spelling and Word Choice

You can use the preview activity to introduce spelling and word choice. Students can then complete the unit in class or for homework. Additional exercises appear on the Companion Website.

Preview

EDIT SPELLING

Work with a partner and read the sentences. Underline and correct three spelling errors in each sentence.

1. In the <u>futur</u>, I <u>realy</u> want to remain in perfect <u>healt</u>, so I will exercise a lot.
   (future, really, health)

2. We <u>tought</u> that the <u>appartement</u> was <u>beautifull</u>, so we rented it for our family.
   (thought, apartment, beautiful)

3. He often talks about <u>interresting</u> <u>sujects</u> <u>whit</u> me, and I love to listen to him.
   (interesting, subjects, with)

4. They <u>finaly</u> opened their new <u>restaurent</u>, but they had many <u>problemes</u>.
   (finally, restaurant, problems)

5. Please send an <u>exemple</u> of your <u>writting</u> to the human resources department at this <u>adresse</u>.
   (example, writing, address)

Spelling: Forms and Usage

ADDING PREFIXES AND SUFFIXES

Add a **prefix** to the beginning of a word in order to change the word's meaning. Be careful when the last letter of the prefix is the same as the first letter of the main word.

mis + spell = misspell   ir + responsible = irresponsible

Add a **suffix** to the end of a word in order to change the word's meaning. When you add the suffix –ly to a word ending in –l, keep the original l. If the word ends in –e, keep the –e, then add the –ly.

real + ly = really   sure + ly = surely

SOME COMMONLY MISSPELLED WORDS

You can find a more comprehensive list of misspelled words in *Avenues 2: Grammar Review Guide*.

address	future	reasonable
alcohol	government	recommend
apartment	health	resource
business	height	responsible
career	human	restaurant
company	immediately	school
course	interesting	separate
developed	medicine	succeed
embarrassed	ninth	success
environment	park	technology
example	personality	visit
exercise	problem	which
family	questioned	with

Word Choice: Forms and Usage

PREPOSITIONS OF TIME AND PLACE

	PREPOSITIONS OF TIME		PREPOSITIONS OF PLACE	
in	**in** a year **in** a month **in** the specific period of the day or evening *in* a season	**in** 2005 **in** February **in** the morning/ afternoon/ evening **in** the summer	**in** a city **in** a country **in** a continent	**in** Calgary **in** Japan **in** Africa
on	**on** a day of the week **on** a specific date **on** a specific holiday "**on** time" (meaning "punctual")	**on** Tuesday **on** January 25 **on** Labour Day **on** my birthday **on** time	**on** a specific street **on** a planet **on** a technological device "**on** top"	**on** Main Street **on** Earth **on** TV **on** the radio/ phone/computer **on** top
at	**at** a specific time of day **at** night **at** a meal	**at** 1:30 p.m. **at** night **at** breakfast/ lunch/dinner	**at** a specific address **at** a specific building	**at** 32 Elm Avenue **at** the hotel
from ... to	**from** one time **to** another	**from** 9 a.m. **to** 6 p.m.	**from** one place **to** another	**from** Chile **to** Canada
for	**for** a period of time	**for** two hours	**for** a distance	**for** five kilometres

SOME COMMONLY CONFUSED WORDS

arrive	to appear at a destination	They usually **arrive** at 6 a.m.
happen	to take place; to occur	What **happened**? When did the accident **happen**?
always	a situation exists at all times	You are **always** late.
still	a past situation continues to exist	I am **still** waiting for you!
again	a past action is repeated	The computer crashed **again**.
dead	(adjective) not living	That is a **dead** bird. The cat killed it.
death	(noun) the state of being dead	The **death** of Amy Winehouse was tragic.
die	(verb) to stop living	The bird will **die** if we leave it on the road.
earn	to receive money for working	Rosa **earns** $20 an hour.
win	to finish first with the highest score; to gain a prize in a contest	Jacob **won** the race. They **won** $5000 in the lottery.
fun	(adjective) pleasant (noun) enjoyment; a good time	I had a **fun** trip to Italy. We had **fun** every day.
funny	humorous	Robert is so **funny**! He makes me laugh.
leave	to exit; to go away	I need to **leave** in ten minutes. My boyfriend is waiting for me.
quit	to give up one's job	Graham **quit** his job at Burger King.
learn	to discover new information	I want to **learn** how to cook.
teach	to instruct or give knowledge to	My father will **teach** me how to cook.
say	to express in words (Follow *say* with the actual words that were said)	Lia **said**, "The film is great." Lia **said** that the film is great.
tell	to communicate (Follow *tell* with a noun or pronoun. You *tell* somebody something.)	Lia **told** me that the film is great.
succeed	(verb) to do well in an endeavour	I hope to **succeed** in this course.
success	(noun) achievement	My presentation was a **success**.
watch	view something that moves (action on TV, people walking by)	We will **watch** a movie tonight.
look at	view something that is immobile	I want to **look at** the paintings.
look for	search for	I can't find my keys. I will **look for** them.

Practice

EXERCISE 1 CORRECT SPELLING ERRORS

Underline and correct fifteen spelling errors. See page 90 for a list of commonly misspelled words.

family
EXAMPLE: The <u>familly</u> eats meals together.

1. Online games have changed the <u>environnement</u> that children grow up in. Now,
   environment

   parks
   children don't play in <u>parcs</u>. Instead, they sit in front of a screen and get very

   exercise   success   school
   little <u>exercice</u>. Critics argue that online games affect a child's <u>sucess</u> at <u>scool</u>.

   However, recent research suggests that video games can be beneficial. They

   can help a child's hand-eye coordination. They are also a good way to introduce

   businesses
   a small child to computers. Some <u>buisnesses</u> teach employees new skills with

   resources
   video games. Often, a company's human <u>ressources</u> department organizes

   the courses.

   Humans
2. <u>Humains</u> develop in complicated ways. According to

   interesting
   some <u>interresting</u> research, games stimulate a child's

   developing
   <u>developping</u> brain. Games can have positive effects on

   health
   mental <u>healt</u>. Studies also show that video games can

   government
   help a child release stress. The American <u>governement</u>

   is even spending over US$250 million on educational

   video games.

   problem
3. Everybody knows that sitting in front of a screen can be a <u>probleme</u>, but perhaps

   responsible
   video games can have positive effects if parents are <u>responsable</u> and set limits.

   recommend
   Experts <u>recommand</u> that children spend a maximum of one hour per day in front

   of a video screen. Of course, to have a well-rounded personality, children also

   need to socialize with others.

IN, ON, AND AT

Generally, as the description of a place or time becomes more precise, you move from *in* to *on* to *at*.

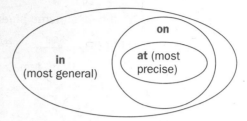

I live **in** Montreal, **on** Duluth Street, **at** 3550.
The meeting is **in** May **on** the 22nd **at** 3 p.m.

TIP

To Versus *At*

Generally use *to* after verbs that indicate movement from one place to another. Use *to* after the following verbs:

   go **to**   walk **to**   run **to**   move **to**   return **to**

Exception: Do not put *to* before *home*.

   I'll go home with you.

Generally use *at* after verbs that indicate stillness. Use *at* after the following verbs:

   wait **at**   stay **at**   sit **at**   look **at**   work **at**

EXERCISE 2 PREPOSITIONS

Fill in the blanks with *in, on, at, for, to,* and *from ... to.* If necessary, refer to the prepositions chart on page 90.

     EXAMPLE: Richard James was born in Philadelphia.

1. Richard James unveiled the "Slinky" to the world _____in_____ 1945 _____in_____ Philadelphia, Pennsylvania. _____At_____ Gimbels, _____on_____ Market Street, hundreds of people bought the first Slinky toys.

2. A year earlier, _____in_____ 1944, James worked on a ship. _____On_____ a Monday _____at_____ 4 o'clock _____in_____ the afternoon, he was building a machine when a coil fell and bounced _____on_____ the ship's deck. The spring appeared to be "walking." _____At_____ dinner that evening, he realized that he could make a new toy for children.

→

3. James worked on his idea _____for_____ six months. Soon after, he and his wife, Betty, started a company and produced Slinky toys. The toy was first sold _____on_____ November 4, 1945.

4. _____In_____ 1960, James suffered an emotional crisis, and he left his wife and six children. He moved _____from_____ the United States _____to_____ Bolivia. He joined a religious group. Betty James stayed _____in_____ the US. She led the company successfully _____for_____ 28 years.

FOR VERSUS TO AND DURING

For Versus To

The infinitive consists of **to** and the verb. Never use **for** in infinitive forms, and never put **for** and **to** together.

>   **to**
> Angela is ready ~~for to~~ leave.

For Versus During

Sometimes people confuse the prepositions **for** and **during** because both indicate that an activity happened over a period of time. However, these words are not interchangeable.

Use **for** to explain *how long* something took to happen. Use **during** to explain *when* it happened.

> The service station closed **for** <u>two hours</u> **during** <u>the blackout</u>.
> The ice-cream store opens **for** <u>three months</u> **during** <u>the summer season</u>.

TIP

Pay For

You <u>pay</u> **for** something.

EXERCISE 3 CORRECT PREPOSITION ERRORS

Underline and correct eight errors in the paragraphs. Look for missing or incorrect prepositions.

>   to
> **EXAMPLE:** We like ^work together.

1. My brother wants ^to patent a new cellphone application. I'm a law student, so he asked me ~~for~~ to give him information about how to obtain a patent. We decided ^to meet ~~for~~ to discuss his options. He was not ready ~~for~~ to see me until March.

2. ~~During~~ For three days last March, we discussed different strategies. We finally decided to register for a patent in Canada, which would give him patent protection ~~during~~ for 20 years. He was willing to pay ^for his patent by himself.

EXERCISE 4 LOCATION PREPOSITIONS

Write the letter of the best definition in the spaces provided.

Prepositions

1. about _____ e
2. above _____ d
3. against _____ g
4. below (under) _____ i
5. behind _____ f
6. between _____ a
7. near _____ h
8. through _____ b
9. toward _____ c

Definitions and Examples

a) (in the middle of two things) Kim sits … Jason and Eric.

b) (to enter a hole or passage and pass to the other side) The ball went … the window.

c) (in the direction of) The race car moved … the finish line.

d) (higher than) The clock is … the door.

e) (regarding a particular topic) The show is … bats. (approximately) It takes … three hours to get there.

f) (in the back of) Don't talk about me … my back.

g) (in competition with) Our team plays … the Raptors. (to lean on an upright surface) The hockey stick is leaning … the wall.

h) (close to, beside) Laval is … Montreal.

i) (in a lower position) The water runs … the bridge.

SOME COMMON PREPOSITIONAL EXPRESSIONS

Many nouns, verbs, and adverbs are usually followed by certain prepositions. Memorize the following prepositional expressions:

afraid (scared) of	consist of	participate in	search for
agree with	depend on	rely on	specialize in
believe in	interested in	responsible for	think about / of

EXAMPLES: Some people don't <u>believe</u> **in** ghosts.

They <u>depend</u> **on** science to answer difficult questions.

Are you <u>interested</u> **in** paranormal events?

TIP

Phrasal Verbs

Some verbs change meaning when different prepositions are added to them. Review the following phrasal verbs and their meanings.

Get		Put	
get along	(have friendly relations)	put on	(place something on)
get up	(awaken)	put away	(put in a proper place)
get into / on	(enter)	put off	(postpone)
get out	(leave)	take off	(remove)

EXERCISE 5 PREPOSITIONS AND PREPOSITIONAL EXPRESSIONS

PART A

Choose the correct preposition in parentheses. Note that *X* means "nothing."

EXAMPLE: I relied (in / on / at) my Rubik's cube to keep my mind active.

1. When I was younger, I did not get (along / in / up) with other children at school. I relied (in / on / X) my older brother for companionship. After school, he was responsible (in / of / for) me. He was very strong and was not afraid (in / on / of) anything.

2. I depended (of / on / at) games to keep my mind active. For example, I loved the Rubik's cube. I bought my first cube when I was eight years old. I paid (X / on / for) it myself. The first time, I played with it (during / on / for) three weeks before I solved it. I would get (in / on / up) early each morning, put (in / on / off) my clothes, and then play with my Rubik's cube. In the evenings, I took (in / on / off) my clothes and put them (off / away / on), and then I went to bed, still holding the cube. I thought (in / on / about) the cube every day.

3. The Rubik's cube was invented (on / in / at) 1974 by Hungarian architecture professor Erno Rubik. It consisted (in / on / of) small coloured blocks. Ideal Toys was interested (in / on / X) the cube.

PART B

Write the correct preposition in the spaces provided.

EXAMPLE: I played with the toy _for_ three hours.

4. There are many Rubik's cube competitions around the world. The next World Rubik's Cube Championship will occur next year _____in_____ Bangkok, and it will last _____for_____ three days. I will participate _____in_____ the competition. I will get _____on_____ a plane and go _____to_____ the competition. I will be responsible _____for_____ the cost of the flight. I will also pay _____for_____ the hotel room.

5. Every day, I plan to get _____up_____ at 8 a.m., put _____on_____ a bathing suit and run _____to_____ the beach for a morning swim. In the afternoons, I will see some of the fastest "speed cubers" _____in_____ the world. I am not afraid _____of_____ the competitors. These days, I often think _____about_____ the competition.

SOME, NO, AND ANY

Use **some** in affirmative sentences and **no** in negative sentences. Use **any** in sentences that contain "not" or the contraction "n't." In questions, you can use *some* or *any*.

> I would like **some** help. I don't need **any** money. Can you give me **some/any** advice?

Also use **any** to mean "it doesn't matter which."

> I can meet you **any** time. I'll go to **any** restaurant.

EXERCISE 6 SOME, NO, AND ANY

PART A

Write *some*, *any*, or *no* in the spaces provided.

1. _____Some_____ people have addictions to their mobile phones. They'll buy _____any_____ new phone or application that comes on the market.

2. The first cellphone was invented by Dr. Martin Cooper in 1973. It really had _____no_____ resemblance to the phones we use today. It was huge and weighed about two kilograms. Cooper believed that people wanted access to a phone in _____any_____ setting.

3. In 1984, my parents didn't want to spend _____any_____ money on a cellphone. But of course, these days, they have _____no_____ problem paying for a cellphone.

PART B

Write *something*, *anything*, or *nothing* in the spaces provided.

4. Personally, I haven't bought _____anything_____ for my phone. I always get calls from the phone company, trying to sell me _____something_____, but there is _____nothing_____ about the new smart phones that interests me. I don't want to have access to the Internet all day because I would do _____nothing_____ except surf the Net!

PART C

Write *somebody*, *nobody*, or *anybody* in the spaces provided.

5. Yesterday, I went to work, but _____nobody_____ was there. I didn't see _____anybody_____. I yelled out, "Is _____somebody / anybody_____ there?" _____Nobody_____ answered, so I knew that I was alone. Then when I arrived home, there wasn't _____anybody_____ in the house! I spent the entire day alone.

AVOID DOUBLE NEGATIVES

A **double negative** occurs when you combine a negative word such as *no*, *nothing*, *nobody*, or *nowhere* with a negative adverb such as *not*, *never*, *rarely*, or *seldom*. The result is a sentence that has a double negative meaning. Such sentences can be confusing because the negative words cancel each other out. There are two ways to correct double negatives. Either remove one of the negative words, or change *no* to *any*.

Double Negative	Corrections
She **doesn't give no** interviews.	She **doesn't give** interviews.
	She **gives no** interviews.
	She **doesn't give any** interviews.

EXERCISE 7 CORRECT DOUBLE NEGATIVES

Identify and correct eight double negatives in the paragraphs. You can correct each error in more than one way.

any   had
EXAMPLE: He didn't have ~~no~~ close friends.   OR   He ~~didn't have~~ no close friends.

1. Steve Jobs co-founded Apple Inc. in 1976. At the time, many people in the

    saw no or didn't see any
    computer business <u>didn't see no</u> commercial future for a personal computer,

    paid no or didn't pay any
    and most companies <u>didn't pay no</u> attention to Steve Jobs.

    had no or didn't have any
2. Jobs <u>didn't have no</u> special training when he started his company. Also, Steve

    had no or didn't have any
    Jobs <u>didn't have no</u> money. In fact, he had to sell his Volkswagen Minibus just

    to get his new company started.

3. Jobs was actually kicked out of Apple in the mid-1980s.

    had nothing or didn't have anything
    At that time, many people at Apple <u>didn't have nothing</u> nice

    to say about Jobs. They complained that he was erratic and

    undependable. Jobs returned to Apple in 1997. When he

    nobody had or nobody had any
    returned, <u>nobody had no</u> complaints about him. Steve Jobs

    died in 2011. Apple may or may not continue to be successful.

    don't know anything or know nothing
    Investors <u>don't know nothing</u> about the future. Personally, I don't

    any
    care about Apple. I rarely have <u>no</u> contact with Apple computers.

REALLY AND VERY

Both *really* and *very* mean "extremely." Put **really** before adjectives, adverbs, and verbs.

It is **really** <u>hot</u>. He runs **really** <u>quickly</u>. I **really** <u>love</u> sports.

Put **very** before adjectives and adverbs.

He works **very** <u>hard</u>. He is **very** <u>tired</u>.

Do <u>not</u> put *very* before a verb!

   really
I ~~very~~ like that movie.

TIP

Listen To and *Watch*

Generally put *to* after *listen*. Note: You do not *listen to* TV or movies. You *watch* them!

              watch
I **listen** **to** music. I also love to ~~listen to~~ movies.

EXERCISE 8 CHOOSE THE CORRECT WORD

Underline the correct word in parentheses. If you are not sure of your answer, review the list of commonly confused words on page 91 and previous tips in this unit.

1. When I was a child, I rarely listened (X / at / <u>to</u>) my parents. I (<u>always</u> / still / again) (listened / <u>watched</u>) horror movies on television, and (anybody / <u>nobody</u>) stopped me. My parents tried to (learn / <u>teach</u>) me about healthy limits, but I didn't listen (X / at / <u>to</u>) (nothing / <u>anything</u>) that they (<u>said</u> / told).

2. One night, when I was sixteen years old, a frightening thing (arrived / <u>happened</u>). I was home alone while my parents were camping. I was in my bedroom when I heard a noise. (Nobody / <u>Somebody</u> / Anybody) was walking in the kitchen! I (<u>really</u> / very) wanted to scream, but I knew that (<u>nobody</u> / anybody) would hear me. I grabbed my cellphone, and I hid inside my closet. I dialed 911 and I (spoke / <u>told</u>) the operator about my situation.

3. A minute later, I heard a man talking to himself and opening drawers. He just wouldn't (quit / <u>leave</u>) the house! I was really afraid (<u>of</u> / at / X) him. I was not having (<u>fun</u> / funny)! I didn't want to (<u>die</u> / dead / death), so I stayed completely silent. I waited (during / <u>for</u>) about fifteen minutes. I kept thinking (on / in / <u>about</u>) my own (dead / die / <u>death</u>).

→

4. I was (again / <u>still</u> / always) in the closet when I heard the front door close.
    Right after that, the police (happened / <u>arrived</u>). The thief had taken our
    laptops and my mother's jewellery. A week later, the police (<u>said</u> / told) that
    they had found the robber.

5. After that incident, I never watched a horror movie (still / <u>again</u> / always).
    Sometimes, I (always / <u>still</u> / again) have nightmares about that night.

MORE COMMONLY CONFUSED WORDS

Succeed* Versus *Success

Be careful: *succeed* is a verb and *success* is a noun.

            succeed
I wanted to ~~success~~.

Win* Versus *Earn

When you work, you *earn* money. You do not *win* it.

    earn
I ~~win~~ $15 an hour at my job.

Quit* Versus *Leave

You do not *quit* a person or a place. You *quit* a job.

        left
Sarah ~~quit~~ me for another man! I was so upset, I quit my job.

EXERCISE 9 WRITE THE CORRECT WORD

Fill in the blanks with one of the terms in parentheses. Make sure that you use the
correct tense.

1. (*earn, win, quit, leave*)

    Brenda Martin designs hair extensions. In 2005, she competed in a young
    entrepreneur contest, but she didn't _____win_____ any prizes.
    Then she decided to go on the *Dragons' Den*. In the show, people pitch ideas
    for an invention to a group of potential investors. In 2008, Martin had to
    _____leave_____ after her idea was rejected. The "dragons" did not
    think that they could _____earn_____ money with her idea. Martin
    was not discouraged. The following year, Martin's company did well, and she
    _____earned_____ more than $100,000. Eventually, she was able
    to _____quit_____ her day job.

2. (*arrive, happen, succeed, success*)

    A great thing _____happened_____ to Martin after she left the
    show. Many viewers saw her product and ordered it. She managed to

_____ succeed _____ without the help of investors. Today, her

business is a great _____ success _____. Yesterday, do you know

what _____ happened _____? One of Martin's hair extensions

_____ arrived _____ in the mail for my sister.

To practise spelling, read students some of the words from the spelling list on page 90 and ask them to spell the words.

Answer the following questions. If you don't know an answer, go back and review the appropriate section.

Correct twelve errors in the underlined words. Write C above the five correct words.

1. Marissa moved <u>at</u> [to] Montreal <u>on</u> [C] September 1, 2010, and she <u>always</u> [still] lives there.

2. She found an <u>appartement</u> [apartment] <u>on</u> [C] Jeanne-Mance Street.

3. Her <u>adress</u> [address] is simple: she lives <u>on</u> [at] 5050 Jeanne-Mance.

4. She takes some <u>cours</u> [courses] at university, and her professors <u>learn</u> [teach] her many things.

5. She <u>very</u> [really] likes to study. She will study <u>during</u> [for] three more years.

6. She is a very <u>responsable</u> [responsible] person, and we know she will <u>success</u> [succeed] at <u>school</u> [C].

7. When she finishes her education, she wants to work in <u>human</u> [C] <u>ressources</u> [resources] for a large <u>company</u> [C].

COMPANION **WEB+**
Need more practice?
Visit the Companion Website and try additional exercises about spelling and word choice.

Final Review

You can use the Final Review as a test. There are twenty-five answers in Part A and five answers in Part B for a total of thirty points. You can also find additional practice exercises and testing material on the Companion Website.

PART A

Choose the correct word in parentheses.

1. A few years ago, my father paid (in / X / <u>for</u>) a video-game system. My little brother Max became addicted. He (<u>always</u> / again / still) played video games. Our parents didn't put (no / <u>any</u>) restrictions on Max's playing time. Most days, (anything / <u>nothing</u> / something) would stop Max from playing (during / <u>for</u>) hours. He depended (of / at / <u>on</u>) video games for all of his entertainment.

2. For example, (in / on) May 16, 2009, he received Grand Theft Auto for his birthday. Max played it before dinner, then he ate, and then he played it (still / again / always) after dinner. In fact, when I went to bed that night (in / on / at) 11 p.m., he was (still / again / always) playing.

3. The next day, he played video games constantly (for / during) six hours. When I (listened / watched) him play, I could not look (to / at) some of the scenes. The game was (teaching / learning) him to shoot and kill people. Children do not learn (nothing / anything) useful from Grand Theft Auto.

4. I (said / told) my parents about the violence in the game. "The game is full of (dead / death / died) and destruction," I shouted. "The goal is to kill, and children see many (died / dead / death) bodies! The games are (responsable / responsible) for some of the violence in the world."

5. My parents didn't believe me. My father (told / said) that video games are a (fun / funny) way to relieve stress and socialize with others. Then my parents laughed at me for being so serious, but I said that it wasn't (fun / funny)!

6. I was so angry that I (quit / left) the house, and I stayed at my friend's house (during / for) a few days. I (very / really) questioned my parents' decisions. But I must admit that my brother is not violent today. Maybe the game had no lasting effect on him.

PART B

Underline and correct five spelling errors in the paragraph.

7. I have a normal familly^{family}. My mother is a doctor, so she makes sure that we are in excellent health. We try to exercice^{exercise} every day, and we eat well. My father has his own business, and it is a great sucess^{success}. He has a very friendly personnality^{personality}, so people love to work with him. My father recommands^{recommends} that I study in commerce, but I have my own plans. In the future, I would prefer to work as a musician.

You can ask students to remove this page and hand it in. In the students' books, pages are perforated.

SPEAKING AND WRITING

Students can do the writing exercise on a separate sheet of paper. Ask them to exchange sheets with another team and peer edit for correct spelling, prepositions, and word choice.

My home

Work with a partner. Tell your partner about the layout of a room in your house or apartment. Your partner will write down the key features. Afterwards, write what your partner tells you. Then review your prepositions, spelling, and word choice.

UNIT 9

Adjectives and Adverbs

Use the Preview activity to introduce comparative and superlative forms of adjectives and adverbs.

Preview

WHAT ARE ADJECTIVES AND ADVERBS?

Adjectives give information about nouns (people, places, and things). **Adverbs** modify verbs.

adjectives before the noun   adverb

He is an **intelligent** and **handsome** <u>man</u>.   He <u>works</u> **quickly**.

Adjectives have comparative forms (ending in –*er*) and superlative forms (ending in –*est*).

He is **nicer than** me. I am **meaner than** he is. He is **the nicest** person I know.

TRANSPORTATION

Work with a partner to compose sentences. Write five sentences comparing the different transportation methods below. Indicate which of the following methods is better, worse, the fastest, etc.

bike   car   subway   train   airplane

EXAMPLE: A bike is cheaper than a car.

1. _____

_____

2. _____

_____

3. _____

_____

4. _____

_____

5. _____

_____

Adjectives and Adverbs: Forms and Usage

ADJECTIVES

ADJECTIVE FORM

Adjectives are always singular, even if the nouns they modify are plural.

beautiful large
Our city has ~~beautifuls larges~~ parks.

ADJECTIVE PLACEMENT

Adjectives appear *before* the nouns they modify or after linking verbs such as *be*, *look*, *feel*, and *seem*.

before the noun *man*
The **angry young** <u>man</u> was in trouble with the law.

after the verb *be*
The man <u>was</u> **angry** and **passionate**.

COMPARATIVE AND SUPERLATIVE FORMS OF ADJECTIVES

		COMPARATIVE	SUPERLATIVE
Add –*er* or –*est* to one-syllable adjectives.	short	short**er than**	**the** short**est**
When the adjective ends in a consonant-vowel-consonant, double the last letter.	thin	thin**ner than**	**the** thin**nest**
In two-syllable adjectives ending in a consonant + *y*, change *y* to *i* and add –*er* or –*est*.	happy	happ**i**er than	**the** happ**i**est
Add *more* or *most* to adjectives of two or more syllables.	modern	**more** modern than	**the** most **modern**
Irregular adjectives have special forms.	good bad little* far	**better than** **worse than** **less than** **farther than**	**the best** **the worst** **the least** **the farthest**

* Meaning "a small amount."

ADVERBS

Adverbs give information about verbs. Most adverbs end in –*ly*. Some exceptions are the adverbs *fast*, *high*, *far*, *late*, *often*, and *soon*, which never end in –*ly*.

adjective	→	adverb	adjective	→	adverb
nice		nice**ly**	careful		careful**ly**
clear		clear**ly**	beautiful		beautiful**ly**

Lady Gaga plays the piano **quickly**.

(The adverb *quickly* describes the action of playing.)

COMPARATIVE AND SUPERLATIVE FORMS OF ADVERBS

		COMPARATIVE	SUPERLATIVE
Add *more* or *most* to adverbs that end in *–ly*.	quickly slowly	**more** quickly **than** **more** slowly **than**	**the most** quickly **the most** slowly
Some adverbs have special forms.	fast often well badly	**faster than** **more** often **than** **better than** **worse than**	**the fastest** **the most** often **the best** **the worst**

EQUALITY: *AS ... AS* AND *THE SAME AS*

Both **as ... as** and **the same as** express equality.

> I am **as tall as** you.
> My car is **the same colour as** your car.
> I can run **as quickly as** you can.

Sometimes one object is **not as** "equal" **as** another.

> Bicycles are **not as dangerous as** skateboards.

Practice

TIP

Adjective or Noun?

A noun may act like an adjective when it modifies another noun. Remember that adjectives are always singular.

> Those jeans cost fifty **dollars**.
> (*Dollars* is a noun.)

> Those are fifty-**dollar** jeans.
> (*Dollar* acts as an adjective and modifies *jeans*.)

EXERCISE 1 IDENTIFY ERRORS

In each sentence, the final noun and adjective(s) are in italics. Underline the final noun. Then correct the error in the adjective's form and/or word order.

EXAMPLE: He is a *person simples*. — simple person

1. John Francis has seen many *environmentals accidents*. — environmental
2. In 1971, he saw a major *oils spill*. — oil
3. At the time, he was a *twenty-five-years-old man*. — twenty-five-year-old
4. The sight gave him some *ideas unusuals*. — unusual ideas
5. He decided to walk to *others cities*. — other
6. He walked for *five years and a half*. — five-and-a-half years
7. He is a *person very active*. — very active person
8. On TedTV, he made a *presentation popular*. — popular presentation

EXERCISE 2 COMPARATIVE AND SUPERLATIVE FORMS OF ADJECTIVES

Write the comparative and superlative forms of the following adjectives.

		Comparative Form	Superlative Form
EXAMPLE:	short	shorter than	the shortest
1.	famous	more famous than	the most famous
2.	good	better than	the best
3.	easy	easier than	the easiest
4.	bad	worse than	the worst
5.	happy	happier than	the happiest
6.	tired	more tired than	the most tired
7.	big	bigger than	the biggest
8.	talented	more talented than	the most talented

EXERCISE 3 COMPARATIVE AND SUPERLATIVE FORMS

Write either the comparative or superlative forms of the words in parentheses. Remember to also write *than* or *the*.

EXAMPLE: One of (new) the newest popular art forms is graffiti.

1. Graffiti artists have to be (careful) _____ more careful than _____ other artists because their art form is illegal. Many people hate graffiti and think it is (bad) _____ worse than _____ other types of art. For example, business owner Maurice W. says that graffiti artists are (bad) _____ the worst _____ of all the artists because they damage people's property.

2. Peter Gibson, also known as "Roadsworth," is (strange) _____ stranger than _____ many artists. In his early graffiti projects, he turned Montreal crosswalks into giant zippers. When he started painting graffiti, he was (fast) _____ faster than _____ other artists. His artwork was also (political) _____ more political than _____ the work of other artists. For example, in 2001, he spray-painted cyclist symbols on roads because he thought that Montreal didn't have enough bicycle lanes.

© ERPI • REPRODUCTION PROHIBITED

3. Today, Roadsworth is probably (famous) _____the most famous_____

graffiti artist in Montreal. Perhaps he is respected because his ideas are

(good) _____better than_____ the ideas of most Canadian

graffiti artists. He is also (talented) _____more talented than_____

many others.

4. These days, the Quebec government pays Roadsworth to produce public art.

Some people believe that his art is (good) _____the best_____

street art in Canada.

TIP

Adverbs

Modify an action verb with an **adverb**. Most adverbs end in *–ly*.

    more slowly
Kevin paints ~~slower~~ than I do.

EXERCISE 4 ADJECTIVE OR ADVERB?

Decide if the italicized word is an adjective or an adverb. If it's an adverb, add *–ly* when necessary. If the word doesn't require an *–ly*, put an X in the space.

  EXAMPLE: She works very *efficient* _ly_ .

1. In the past, Kathleena Howie-Garcia was an extremely *serious*__X__
graffiti artist. Using the tag "Lady K Fever," she worked *careful*__ly__.
Spraying walls in Vancouver and Toronto, she *often*__X__ made her
artwork at night. She could paint a wall *quick*__ly__.

2. In 2001, she became *extreme*__ly__ creative. She went to New York,
and she became a *serious*__X__ artist. She painted *beautiful*__ly__.

3. Since 2004, her work has been very *successful*__X__. *She* has
*successful*__ly__ completed many public art projects. She has
become *firm*__ly__ established as a great graffiti artist.

COMPARATIVE AND SUPERLATIVE FORMS OF ADVERBS

Most adverbs have two or more syllables. Use *more* and *the most* to form comparatives and superlatives.

She painted walls **more quickly than** other artists.

She works **the most carefully** of all the local artists.

EXERCISE 5 COMPARATIVE FORMS

Use the comparative forms of the following adjectives and adverbs. You may have to turn an adjective into an adverb by adding –ly. Remember that an adverb describes an action and an adjective describes a person, place, or thing.

EXAMPLES: Quebec is (quiet) <u>quieter</u> than Montreal.
Clara works (quiet) <u>more quietly</u> than I do.

1. Living in the city and living in the suburbs are two very different experiences.

   City life is (busy) _____ busier _____ than suburban life.

   I am (nervous) _____ more nervous _____ in a city than in a suburb.

   On the other hand, it is (easy) _____ easier _____ to get around

   in cities because there is a lot of public transportation. People can move

   around (quick) _____ more quickly _____ in cities than in suburbs.

   When I am in Montreal, I drive (careful) _____ more carefully _____ than

   I do in Kirkland.

2. Suburban people are (nice) _____ nicer _____

   to strangers than city people are. City people treat strangers

   (harsh) _____ more harshly _____ than suburban

   people do. Suburban people say "hello" to their neighbours

   (frequent) _____ more frequently _____ than city

   people do.

3. However, in some ways, people who live in cities are (lucky)

   _____ luckier _____ than those who live

   in suburbs. Cities generally have more movie theatres,

   museums, and music clubs. For entertainment, cities are

   (good) _____ better _____ than suburbs. People

   can have fun (easy) _____ more easily _____

   in a big city than in a suburb. Sometimes, a suburb is (bad)

   _____ the worst _____ place to be on a

   Saturday night.

TIP

Equality: *As ... As* and *The Same As*

Use **as ... as** and **the same as** to express equality. Do not use *than*.

as

The bus is as fast ~~than~~ the subway.

EXERCISE 6 ADJECTIVES AND ADVERBS

Write the correct forms of the adjectives and adverbs. You may need to change an adjective to an adverb. You will also need to add the following words: *the*, *than*, or *as ... as*.

> **EXAMPLE:** Elsa Womak is (old) _the oldest_ person in her city. However, she is not _as old as_ her sister Mabel.

1. When he was young, Rajiv was a good athlete, but he started smoking when he was thirteen. When he was a child, his lungs were much (healthy) _____ _____ _healthier than_ _____ they are today. These days, he can't run (quick) _____ _as quickly as_ _____ he used to.

2. In past decades, smokers didn't have (many restrictions) _____ _____ _as many restrictions as_ _____ they have today. They smoked (free) _____ _more freely than_ _____ they do these days. They could smoke at work, in restaurants, and in all other public places. Smoking was one of (popular) _____ _the most popular_ _____ activities for people. On the other hand, the workplace environment wasn't (pleasant) _____ _as pleasant as_ _____ it is today. The health of non-smokers was (bad) _____ _worse than_ _____ it is today. My dad's office was one of (smoky) _____ _the smokiest_ _____ places in our city. These days, workplace conditions are much (good) _____ _better than_ _____ they were in the past.

TIP

Than or *Then*?

In comparisons, use *than*. Do not use *then*, which means "next" or "after that."

>   **than**
> France is smaller ~~then~~ Canada.

EXERCISE 7 IDENTIFY ERRORS

Underline and correct the errors in the following sentences. If the sentence is correct, write *C* beside it.

>   ~~more~~
> **EXAMPLE:** This office is <u>more</u> cleaner than that one.

1. Mexico City has more people <u>then</u> all of Canada.
              than

2. Canada is a <u>more</u> younger country than Mexico. ➔
      ~~more~~

3. Toronto is not as busy ~~than~~ *as* Mexico City.

4. Quebec City is one of the oldest settlements in North America. C

5. Mexico's road to independence was ~~more~~ *more* harder than Canada's.

6. Unfortunately, Mexico City is not as safe ~~than~~ *as* Toronto.

7. The violent drug war raging in Mexico is possibly the ~~sadder~~ *saddest* ongoing conflict in the world.

8. Hopefully, the situation in Mexico won't become ~~worser~~ *worse* than it is right now.

9. Does Mexico have a ~~more~~ *more* better cultural history than Canada does?

10. Some people can learn Spanish ~~easier~~ *more easily* than English.

↻ UNIT Review

Answer the following questions. If you don't know an answer, go back and review the appropriate section.

1. Write the comparative and superlative forms of the following adjectives and adverbs.

	Comparative Form	Superlative Form
a) good	better than	the best
b) bad	worse than	the worst
c) cute	cuter than	the cutest
d) carefully	more carefully than	the most carefully

2. Underline and correct each error.

a) Bill is a <u>more</u> better businessman than Donald.

Delete *more.*

b) Your situation is not the same <u>than</u> mine is.

as

c) If you complain, it will make things <u>worst</u> than before.

worse

d) Sandra has as much money <u>than</u> I do.

as

e) What is the <u>baddest</u> thing that you have ever done?

worst

Final Review

PART A

Write the correct form of the words in parentheses. You may need to change an adjective to an adverb. You will also need to supply the words *the* or *than*. Do **not** use *as ... as*.

EXAMPLE: Which country has (good) _the best_ legal system in the world today?

1. The US prison system is much (large) _____larger than_____ Canada's. American courts tend to put people in prison (quick) _____ _____more quickly than_____ Canadian courts do. In the world, which nation has (bad) _____the worst_____ prison system?

2. For criminals, Canadian courts are (good) _____better than_____ _____ American courts. These days, the US has one of (high) _____the highest_____ incarceration rates in the world. According to *The New York Times*, the United States has 5 percent of the world's population, but almost 25 percent of the world's prisoners.

3. In the 1980s, the US prison population exploded when that country started building private prisons. Building prisons can be (profitable) _____ _____more profitable than_____ building offices.

4. Many people say that private prisons are much (bad) _____worse than_____ public prisons. They make a profit off the inmates' cheap labour. According to some people, private prisons are (cheap) _____cheaper than_____ _____ public prisons, but they are not as effective.

5. Should Canada build more prisons? American laws are (severe) _____more severe than_____ _____ Canadian laws. Which country has (good) _____the best_____ _____ prison system?

PART B

Underline and correct errors in the sentences. Write *C* beside the sentences that
are correct.

                                                     than
EXAMPLE: You are more stubborn <u>then</u> I am.

                        worse
6. Are public prisons <u>worst</u> than private prisons?

                                easily
7. Americans go to jail more <u>easier</u> than Canadians do.

8. Iranian prisons are not the same as Canadian prisons. C

                            ~~more~~
9. Is the US justice system <u>more</u> better than the Canadian

   justice system?

                                    as
10. Capital punishment is not as effective <u>than</u> some

   people believe.

Compare Items

Working with a partner, choose one of the following topics. Then write six sentences.
Write two comparative and two superlative sentences, and write two sentences
expressing equality.

1. children and adults   4. two technological items

2. two celebrations   5. two sports

3. junk food and health food   6. two seasons

      EXAMPLE: Topic: weddings and funerals

         Comparative: Weddings are happier than funerals.
         Superlative: My brother's wedding was the biggest I have ever seen.
         Equality: My brother is as nice as his wife.

_____

_____

_____

_____

_____

_____

_____

Conditionals

You can use the Preview activity to introduce the concept of conditionals. Write students' ideas on the board.

Preview

WHAT ARE CONDITIONALS?

Conditional sentences suggest a possibility or probability.

> If I **had** a lot of money, I **would buy** a car.

NON-STOP TALKING

Work with a partner or team. One speaker at a time, talk about one of the situations without stopping. You can switch topics at any time. When your teacher flicks the light switch in the classroom, change speakers.

> **EXAMPLE:** What would you do if your best friend stole a diamond ring?
> If my friend stole a ring, I would ask her why she did it. Then I would …

1. What would you do if your boyfriend or girlfriend cheated on you?

2. What would you do if you saw your twelve-year-old sister smoking cigarettes?

3. What would you do if your friend drank too much wine and was getting into his car?

4. What would you do if your very old dog started having "accidents" all over the house?

5. What two things do you wish you had done when you were in high school?

Conditionals: Forms and Usage

Conditional sentences describe an action and its consequences. Such sentences have two parts; the **main clause (the result)** depends on the condition set in the *if* **clause (the condition)**.

If clause (the condition)	Main clause (the result)
If you work hard,	you will succeed.
If I won the lottery,	I would buy a house.
If she had studied,	she would have passed the test.

POSSIBLE PRESENT OR FUTURE

Use the **possible** form when the present condition is true or the future condition is very possible.

If + present tense	present or future tense
If you **need** money,	there **is** some on the table. (This present situation is **true**.)
If you **ask** for help,	I **will help** you. (This will **probably** happen.)

UNLIKELY PRESENT

Use the **unlikely** form when the condition is not likely and probably won't happen.

If + past tense	*would* (expresses an intention)
	could (expresses a possibility)
If I **won** money in the lottery,	I **would buy** a horse.
If Eva **knew** how to speak Spanish,	she **could take** the job.

IMPOSSIBLE PAST

To help students understand the past perfect, you could ask them to do the past perfect exercise in Appendix 2, on page 152.

Use the **impossible past** when the condition cannot happen because the event is over. The speaker expresses regret about the past event or a wish that the past event had worked out differently.

If + past perfect tense	*would have* + past participle
	could have + past participle
If you **had invited** me,	I **would have come** to your party.
If he **had known** about the rainstorm,	he **could have brought** an umbrella.

Note: The past perfect tense is formed with *had* + the past participle. To learn more about the past perfect tense, see Appendix 2, page 152.

TIP

If Clauses Can Be Reversed

Conditional sentences can begin or end with an **if clause**. Place a comma after the **if clause** when this clause begins a sentence. Do not use a comma when a sentence ends with an **if clause**.

If clause at beginning:	**If he found a job**, Sam would move.
If clause at end:	Sam would move **if he found a job**.

Practice

EXERCISE 1   POSSIBLE SITUATIONS

The sentences below express *possible* situations. Fill in the blanks with either the present or future tense.

EXAMPLE: If he (arrive) _arrives_ on time, he will join the demonstration.

1. Tomorrow, there (be) _____will be_____ a protest downtown. If it (rain) _____rains_____, I will not go. If it (be) _____is_____ sunny, many people (shout) _____will shout_____ in the streets.

2. People are angry with the government. If I (have) _____have_____ the time to prepare, I (make) _____will make_____ a sign. If nobody (go) _____goes_____ tomorrow, it (be) _____will be_____ disappointing. If enough people (be) _____are_____ politically active, they (make) _____will make / can make_____ a difference.

UNLIKELY CONDITIONALS

Using *Would*

In **unlikely present** sentences, put **would** only in the main clause (the result). Generally, do not put *would* in the *if* clause (the condition).

     helped
If you ~~would help~~, we would finish more quickly.

Using *Were*

In **unlikely conditional** sentences, when the *if* clause contains *be*, always use **were** even when the subject is *I*, *he*, *she*, or *it*. In **informal speech**, you may hear **was** in the *if* clause.

Formal usage: If I **were** you, I **would stop** smoking.

Informal usage: If I **was** you, I **would stop** smoking.

EXERCISE 2 UNLIKELY SITUATIONS

Complete the sentences below, using the appropriate tense of the verbs provided. Each sentence expresses an unlikely situation.

    EXAMPLE: Gabriel is a workaholic.
              If he worked less, he (have) more fun.   _____would have_____

1. If Gabriel (treat) others nicely, he would have more friends.   _____treated_____

2. He (be) a lot healthier if he exercised more often.   _____would be_____

3. If he (can), he would quit his job.   _____could_____

4. Amanda (move) into his apartment if he asked her.   _____would move_____

5. If Gabriel won the lottery, he (travel) to Barbados.   _____would travel_____

6. If he (be) more mature, he would receive more respect.   _____were_____

7. Gabriel's life (improve) if he changed his attitude.   _____would improve_____

EXERCISE 3 POSSIBLE FUTURE AND UNLIKELY PRESENT

In each of the following sentences, choose the correct form of the verb. Decide if the situation is possible or unlikely. Use either the possible future or the unlikely present conditional forms.

> **EXAMPLE:** If you (knew) _knew_ her, you would like her.

1. In sports, repeated head injuries can cause memory loss and symptoms of Parkinson's and Alzheimer's diseases. Some children's football leagues allow full contact. If I were a school administrator, I (allow, not) _would not allow_ _____ students to play tackle football. It is too dangerous for children.

2. My son loves football. Next year, if he joins his school's tackle-football team, I (worry) _will worry_ about him. If his school had a flag-football team, it (be) _would be_ _____ better for the children, but the school doesn't have such a team. I (feel) _would feel_ much better if my son didn't like football!

3. If you (have) _had_ a child, what would you do? If your son or daughter (want) _wanted_ to play tackle football, would you permit it?

4. Football coach Ken Rayburn believes that tackling is not dangerous. But if he visited a typical nursing home, he (find, probably) _would probably find_ former football players, boxers, and other athletes with serious mental issues caused by their head injuries. For sure, if I (be) _were_ a football player, I (worry) _would worry_ about head injuries. But I will never play football.

EXERCISE 4 IDENTIFY CONDITIONAL FORMS

Identify the type of conditional sentence. Write *A*, *B*, or *C* in the spaces provided.

A (possible present or future): If you ask me, I will come.
B (unlikely present): If you asked me, I would come.
C (impossible past): If you had asked me, I would have come.

> **EXAMPLE:** If I could, I would travel to Spain. _____B_____

1. If Raul Morales were younger, he would return to school. _____B_____

2. If he had known how difficult it is to make a career in dance, he would have found a different profession. _____C_____

116 | AVENUES 2 | English Grammar

© ERPI • REPRODUCTION PROHIBITED

3. If you want to learn the tango, he will teach it to you. _____A_____

4. According to Morales, the tango is easy to learn if you practise a lot. _____A_____

5. If he had taken better care of himself, he would not have needed knee surgery. _____C_____

6. If he takes it easy, he can give three dance classes a week. _____A_____

7. He would give more classes if his doctor permitted it. _____B_____

8. If he had never danced, he would have felt unfulfilled. _____C_____

9. During my childhood, if my family had had the money, I would have studied dance. _____C_____

TIP

Impossible Past

In "impossible" past sentences, do not use *would have* + the past participle in the *if* clause.

had known
If I ~~would have known~~ you were sick, I **would have visited** you.

EXERCISE 5 IMPOSSIBLE PAST CONDITIONAL FORMS

Complete the following sentences using the impossible past conditional tense.

EXAMPLE: If we (have) _had had_ enough money, we would have spent more time in Japan.

1. On a business trip to Japan, Zachary Field made some cultural-etiquette errors. First, he made eye contact with his hosts and discussed business right away. If he (take) _____ had taken _____ more time for small talk, his hosts would have felt more comfortable. Also, if he had avoided direct eye contact, he (appear) _____ would have appeared _____ less aggressive. Basically, if he (understand) _____ had understood _____ the cultural differences, he would not have insulted his hosts.

2. Roger Axtell is an international business traveller. He has written a book called *Do's and Taboos of Humor Around the World*. If Axtell (travel, not) _____ had not travelled _____ extensively, he would have been unable to write about cultural differences.

3. A few years ago, when Axtell was visiting Saudi Arabia, an important customer grabbed his hand while they were walking. In Saudi Arabia, hand holding is a sign of friendship and respect. If Axtell (pull) _____ had pulled _____ away, he (offend) _____ would have offended _____ his host, but he didn't pull away. Still, if he (know) _____ had known _____ in advance about the hand holding, he (feel, not) _____ would not have felt _____ so uncomfortable.

EXERCISE 6 IDENTIFY ERRORS

Underline and correct the errors in the following conditional sentences.

EXAMPLE: They will discuss the problem if they will have time tomorrow.
(correction above: have)

1. People say, "If you work hard, you will succeeds."
(correction above: succeed)

2. If Chandra could has any career, she would like to be a professional singer.
(correction above: have)

3. Chandra would sing in public if she would have enough talent. Unfortunately, she can't sing very well.
(correction above: had)

4. If she will pay $2000 to Ark Music Factory, someone will write a song and produce a music video for her.
(correction above: pays)

5. If Chandra had the money, the producers will use pitch-correcting software to disguise her off-key singing. Unfortunately, she doesn't have $2000.
(correction above: would)

6. When she was a child, she never told her parents about her passion. Maybe if they would have known about her passion, they would have sent her for singing lessons.
(correction above: had)

EXERCISE 7 CONDITIONAL FORMS

Fill in the blanks with the appropriate conditional tense of the verbs.

Alicia and Hamid plan to travel. This is the discussion that they are having.

1. Alicia: If we (spend) _____ spend _____ two years travelling, how will we pay for it?

2. Hamid: If we ask my uncle, he (find) _____ will find _____ us jobs on a ship.

3. Alicia: If we worked on a ship, (we earn) _____ would we earn _____ a lot of money?

4. Hamid: Yes. If we accepted jobs on a ship, the company (pay) _____ would pay _____ for our room and board.

5. Alicia: I want to visit my grandmother in Mexico. If I (ask) _____ asked _____ her, she would probably let us stay with her.

6. Hamid: But if we spent five months in Mexico, I (need) _____ would need _____ to learn Spanish.

7. Alicia: Last year, if you (listen) _____ had listened _____ during our Spanish classes, you (learn) _____ would have learned _____ a lot!

UNIT Review

Complete the following exercises. If you don't know an answer, go back and review the appropriate section.

1. For each sentence, write the verb *buy* in the correct tense.

   a) I ____will buy____ a bike if I save enough money.

   b) I ____would buy____ a motorcycle if I had a better job.

   c) I ____would have bought____ a car if I had saved enough money.

2. Identify and correct the error in each sentence.

   a) If you <u>would meet</u> Kim, you would like her.   ____met____

   b) I will help you if I <u>will have</u> the time.   ____have____

   c) When we were children, we would have been friends if we <u>would have lived</u> in the same town.   ____had lived____

Need more practice? Visit the Companion Website and try additional exercises.

Final Review

You can use the Final Review as a test. There are fifteen answers. You can also find additional practice exercises and testing material on the Companion Website.

PART A

Read each sentence and circle the appropriate answer.

1. If Nick … enough free time, he will travel across Canada.
   a) will have   (b) has   c) would have   d) had

2. Nick is not in great shape. If he were in better shape, he … the country on his bicycle.
   (a) would cross   b) will cross   c) crosses   d) crossed

3. If he … his bike, it would take about three months to cross the country.
   a) would ride   b) will ride   c) rides   (d) rode

4. Last year, Nick hurt his knee. If he … in better shape, he would have cycled every day.
   a) would have been   b) was   (c) had been   d) would be

5. If I had the energy, I … my bike across the country, too. Unfortunately, like Nick, I am not in great shape.
   (a) would ride   b) will ride   c) ride   d) rode

6. Last year, Scott and Becky completed their ride across Canada. It took them sixteen months. If they had taken a direct route, they … much sooner.
   a) would have finished   b) finished   c) had finished   d) would finish

7. If they save enough money, they … the trip again.
   a) would do   b) will do   c) do   d) did

8. Which place would they skip if they … another cross-country trip?
   a) would make   b) will make   c) make   d) made

9. Becky said that if she … a magician, she would skip Manitoba.
   a) would be   b) will be   c) is   d) were

10. Next year, if a lot of people … up driving and instead commute on bikes, it will help the environment.
    a) would give   b) will give   c) give   d) gave

PART B

Fill in each blank with the appropriate verb form.

   EXAMPLE: If you (take) _took_ a good photo, the company would publish it.

11. Someday, if I (travel) _____ travel _____ across Canada, I will take many photos.

12. If I (know) _____ knew _____ how to speak Dutch, I would live in the Netherlands. Unfortunately, I can't speak Dutch.

13. Fifteen years ago, I travelled alone to India. If I (make) _____ had made _____ a video of that trip, it would have been great. But I didn't have a video camera at that time.

14. If I had had a video camera, I (film) _____ would have filmed _____ my visit to Varanasi. I saw the burning ghats along the Ganges River.

15. If I had enough money, I (return) _____ would / could return _____ to India this year. But I don't have much money.

If I Could ...

Work with a partner. Ask and answer the following questions. Give reasons for your answers. Then, in a paragraph, write about some of your partner's answers.

1. What would you include in your future house? What features would you like it to have?

2. If you could visit either the future or the past, which would you choose?

3. If you could live your life over again, what would you do differently?

4. If you had been alive in 1915, what would you have done for a living?

Sentences and Punctuation

Preview

You can use the Preview activity to introduce the unit. Students may miss some of the mistakes. You can assure them that they will learn how to identify errors as they do the exercises in the unit.

WHAT IS A COMPLETE SENTENCE?

A **complete sentence** has a subject and a verb, and it expresses a complete idea.

Have you seen a crime? I have. It was a frightening experience!

Answers may vary.

IDENTIFY ERRORS

Work with a partner. Identify and correct twenty errors in sentence structure, capitalization, or punctuation.

Every Spring, my friend's have a big party. For example, last april, on a friday night, I went to their party. I was driving home when I saw a police car behind me. I pulled over, I didn't know what I had done. The officer was about twenty years old, she looked like a character on that TV show called *Gossip girl*. However, she was very cold, "you went through the stop sign without stopping" Although, I asked her for mercy, she still gave me a $130 ticket. Later, while I was driving home, I texted my friend and wrote, "The police caught me." Maybe I should'nt text when I drive.

In my town, there are too many stop signs, Especially on Ellis avenue and on the road near the River. The city really need's to stop putting stop signs on every corner.

Sentences: Forms and Usage

To make your writing interesting, you should use a variety of sentence types.

SIMPLE SENTENCE

A **simple sentence** has one independent clause (complete idea).

> He examined the crime scene.

COMPOUND SENTENCE

A **compound sentence** contains two or more independent clauses joined by a coordinating conjunction such as *and*, *but*, *or*, *nor*, or *yet*. You can also combine the sentence's complete ideas with a semicolon. A third way to create a compound sentence is to join the complete ideas with a semicolon and transitional expression such as *furthermore*, *however*, or *therefore*.

> independent clause   independent clause
> He examined the crime scene, **and** he took photographs of the site.

> The jury returned to the courtroom; the criminal watched intently.

> The criminal was guilty; **therefore,** she went to prison.

COMPLEX SENTENCE

A **complex sentence** contains at least one independent clause and one dependent clause. A dependent clause "depends" on another clause in order to be complete. The dependent clause begins with a **subordinator** or a **relative pronoun**.

A **subordinator** joins the secondary idea to the main idea. Some common subordinators are *although*, *because*, *unless*, and *whereas*.

> dependent clause   independent clause
> **Although it is very risky**, police work is exciting.

> independent clause   dependent clause
> Robert learned karate **because he wanted to be physically fit**.

A **relative pronoun** introduces information about a noun or pronoun. The most common relative pronouns are *who*, *whom*, *whose*, *which*, and *that*.

> independent clause   dependent clause
> The lawyer introduced evidence **that was at the crime scene**.

Punctuation and Capitalization: Forms and Usage

APOSTROPHES (')

Apostrophes in Contractions

Use an apostrophe to join a subject and verb together.

> **We're** late. **There's** nothing to eat.

Also use an apostrophe to join an auxiliary with *not*.

> I **can't** come. They **aren't** very friendly.

Apostrophes to Show Ownership

You can add an apostrophe followed by an –s ('s) to nouns to indicate possession.

Dylan is the child of Diane. He is **Diane's** child.

If the noun is plural, put the apostrophe after the –s.

The **boys'** clothes are in the washing machine.

If the noun has an irregular plural form, add –'s.

The **men's** room is down the hall.

COMMAS (,) AND PERIODS (.)

Use a comma

- to separate three or more words in a series; (You can put a comma before the final *and*.)

    The doctor is tall, thin, and gentle.

- after an introductory word, phrase, or idea;

    First, Mr. Chen closed his store.

    A few minutes later, he emptied the safe.

- around an interrupting phrase that gives additional information about the subject;

    Kevin, a student at Victoria College, went through a traffic light.

- with quotations, after an introductory phrase.

    He said, "The light was green."

Use a period

- at the end of a complete sentence;
- with the following titles: *Ms.*, *Mrs.*, *Mr.*, and *Dr.* (Don't put a period after *Miss*.)

COLONS (:) AND SEMICOLONS (;)

Use a colon

- after a complete sentence that introduces a list, or after the words *the following*;

    The course has the following sections: crime, law, and justice.

- after a complete sentence that introduces a quotation;

    Picasso's advice was clear: "Find your passion."

- to introduce an explanation or example;

    Raymond showed the evidence: a glass with fingerprints.

- to separate the hours and minutes in expressions of time.

    The store closed at 12:30 and reopened at 2:00.

Use a semicolon

- to join two independent and related clauses.

    Gandhi was a pacifist; he believed in non-violence.

QUOTATION MARKS (" ")

Use **quotation marks** around direct speech. Capitalize the first word in the quotation, and place the end punctuation inside the closing quotation marks.

In his essay, Harris said, "**The** rioters destroyed many buildings."

He asked, "**When** did the riot start?"

CAPITALIZATION

Always capitalize

- the pronoun *I* and the first word of every sentence;

    The man that **I** met is very nice.

- the days of the week, the months, and holidays;

    Wednesday   **J**uly 13   **L**abour **D**ay

- the names of specific places, such as buildings, streets, parks, public squares, lakes, rivers, cities, provinces, and countries;

    Elk **A**venue   **L**ake **H**uron   **C**algary, **A**lberta

- the names of languages, nationalities, tribes, races, and religions;

    Greek   **M**ohawk   **P**rotestant

- the titles of specific individuals;

    General **D**allaire   **P**rime **M**inister **B**rown   **M**rs. **P**itt

- the titles of specific school courses;

    Physics 201   **E**nglish 101   **B**eginner's **S**panish

- the important words in titles of literary or artistic works.

    On the **R**oad   **F**inal **D**estination   **G**ossip **G**irl

Practice

TIP

Coordinators

You can join complete sentences with the following coordinators. (Note that the coordinator *yet* has a similar meaning to *but*.)

   and   but   or   so   yet

She talked, **but** I didn't believe her.

EXERCISE 1 MAKING COMPOUND SENTENCES

Underline the appropriate coordinator in each compound sentence.

1. Kevin Barbieux calls himself a "social phobic," (but / or / so) he is also extroverted. Barbieux has lived in comfortable surroundings, (so / or / and) he has also lived on the streets. The first time he became homeless was in 1982, (but / or / so) he has a lot of experience with homelessness.

2. Barbieux knew that he could live a selfish life, (but / or / so) he could help others. In 2002, he had access to a computer in a library, (so / but / yet) he started a blog called *The Homeless Guy*. On his blog, he describes the needs of homeless people, (so / but / and) he gives advice to ordinary citizens. For example,

homeless people need a place to store their valuables, (<u>so</u> / or / but) good Samaritans can offer to store their items. Barbieux still struggles with homelessness, (so / <u>yet</u> / or) he remains optimistic.

EXERCISE 2 USING SUBORDINATORS

Fill in the blanks with a subordinating conjunction. Use each subordinating conjunction only once. (Note that in some cases, more than one answer is possible.) The first one has been done for you as an example.

| after | as soon as | even though | until | whereas |
| ~~although~~ | because | unless | when | while |

1. David Chen owns the Lucky Moose store in Toronto. _____Although_____ running a store is difficult, he loves his job. However, in 2009, he had a problem. A thief named Anthony Bennett often visited the store. _____While_____ Bennett was browsing, he always acted suspiciously. One day, Bennett stole a $60 pair of pants. An hour later, he returned to the store. __As soon as / After / When__ Chen saw Bennett, he tackled the thief and tied him up. Then Chen and an employee held Bennett _____until_____ the police arrived. __As soon as / After / When__ the police questioned Chen, the shop owner realized that he had some serious legal problems.

2. _____Even though_____ he was the victim of a robbery, Chen was charged with assault and unlawful confinement. Citizens were shocked. According to laws at that time, a property owner couldn't make a citizen's arrest _____unless_____ the criminal was caught in the process of stealing. _____Because_____ Chen made his citizen's arrest an hour after the theft, it was an illegal act. Chen was charged with a serious crime _____whereas_____ the thief was charged with simple theft only. The thief received a thirty-day jail sentence.

3. Local citizens supported Chen. Luckily for Chen, the judge ruled in his favour. The judge said that Mr. Bennett's return to the store constituted "a continuing theft." Of course, Chen's family was very relieved. They cheered __after / as soon as / when__ they heard the verdict.

THAT AND WHICH

Both **that** and **which** give additional information about things. Generally, use commas to set off clauses that begin with *which*.

The judge made a decision **that was controversial**.

The crime rate, **which peaked in the 1980s**, has fallen in recent years.

EXERCISE 3 USING RELATIVE PRONOUNS

In the spaces provided, write *who*, *that*, *which*, or *whose*. In some cases, more than one answer is possible.

EXAMPLE: Last night, I read a story _____that_____ was true.

1. In the early 1900s, William Sydney Porter wrote stories _____that_____ continue to be popular. Porter was a man _____whose_____ life was difficult. In 1894, he worked at a bank _____that_____ was in Austin, Texas. Porter, _____who_____ was not very organized, had a major problem at the bank.

2. The bank charged Porter with embezzlement. Porter's arrest, _____which_____ ruined his reputation, occurred soon after. Instead of going to jail, he escaped and ran off to Honduras. His wife, _____whose_____ health was very bad, could not join him. He decided _____that_____ he could not live without his wife. Porter's return to the US, _____which_____ happened in 1897, resulted in his imprisonment.

3. Porter, _____who_____ also used the pen name "O. Henry," started writing stories in jail. He often wrote stories _____that_____ described the lives of criminals.

O. Henry

TRANSITIONAL EXPRESSIONS

Transitional expressions show the progression of ideas in an essay. They can be placed at the beginning of sentences, and they can also be used to join two complete ideas.

Begin a sentence: However, the game was over.

Join complete ideas: Ray was losing the fight; however, he kept trying.

Some Common Transitional Expressions

Chronology:	first	second	finally	suddenly
Addition:	additionally	also	furthermore	moreover
Emphasis:	above all	clearly	of course	undoubtedly
Comparison:	however	in contrast	nevertheless	similarly
Conclusion:	in conclusion	in short	therefore	thus
Example:	for instance	in fact	for example	

TIP

Although or *However*

Do not confuse *although* and *however*.

Although is a subordinator that means "even though." Do not put a comma after *although*.

However is a transitional expression. Always put a comma after *however*.

> **Although** she broke the law, she didn't go to jail.
> She broke the law; **however,** she didn't go to jail.
> She broke the law. **However,** she didn't go to jail.

© ERPI • REPRODUCTION PROHIBITED

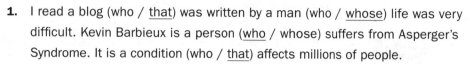

EXERCISE 4 CHOOSING THE RIGHT WORD

Underline the appropriate word in parentheses.

EXAMPLE: I read a story (who / <u>that</u>) was funny.

1. I read a blog (who / <u>that</u>) was written by a man (who / <u>whose</u>) life was very difficult. Kevin Barbieux is a person (<u>who</u> / whose) suffers from Asperger's Syndrome. It is a condition (who / <u>that</u>) affects millions of people.

2. (<u>Although</u> / However) Barbieux was not a professional writer, he decided to start a blog. On his blog, (who / <u>which</u>) he started in 2002, he lists the causes of homelessness. He describes some people with severe mental problems; (although / <u>however</u>), he does not make judgments. According to Barbieux, people (<u>who</u> / which) become homeless have usually had a difficult personal event in their lives. Maybe they have lost their jobs, (<u>or</u> / so) they have had to leave their homes after a divorce.

3. Barbieux describes two types of homeless people: the temporary and the chronic. (<u>Although</u> / However) almost all homeless people have financial problems, some have additional issues. The temporarily homeless live on the streets (because / <u>until</u>) they can find another job. They are homeless for a short period. The chronically homeless are those (<u>who</u> / which) have mental problems or addictions. They may need help; (although / <u>however</u>), they won't always accept it.

 Visit the companion website to practise using *than, then,* and *that.*

COMMONLY CONFUSED WORDS

Whose or Who's?

Who's is the contracted form of *who is.*

 Who's at the door?

Whose indicates possession and replaces *his, her, its,* and *their.*

 Whose bike is that?

Than, Then, and That

Than is used to compare two things: She is older **than** I am.
Then means "at a particular time": He graduated and **then** found a job.
That introduces a clause: The book **that** I read is very good.

TIP

Which

Ensure that you spell *which* correctly.

 which
The prison, ~~wich~~ is now closed, was on an island.

EXERCISE 5 CORRECTING RELATIVE PRONOUNS

Underline and correct ten errors with *who, which, that,* and *whose.* Look for incorrect or misspelled words.

  that
EXAMPLE: Last week, he went to a prison <u>who</u> was on an island.

                                that
1. An interesting story ~~than~~ I read is called "The Cop and the Anthem." The story,
   which
   ~~who~~ was written by O. Henry, is about a homeless man. In the story, Soapy, ~~whose~~
                                                                              who's

→

UNIT 11 | Sentences and Punctuation | 127

© ERPI • REPRODUCTION PROHIBITED

trying to get arrested, doesn't want to spend the winter on a cold park bench.

Each winter, Blackwell Island Penitentiary, ~~who~~ which is an old prison, provides Soapy

with a warm bed.

2. The city of New York, ~~wich~~ which needed a prison, bought the island from the Blackwell

family in 1836. The city built a penitentiary ~~than~~ that opened in 1852. The prison,

~~wich~~ which housed petty criminals, had more than two hundred cells. Most prisoners

~~who's~~ whose crimes were minor enjoyed getting out of the cold. In 1934, the prison

became a hospital ~~than~~ that is still open today. O. Henry, ~~who's~~ whose own life was fascinating,

often wrote about criminals and the homeless.

COMMON SENTENCE ERRORS

Fragments

A **fragment** is an incomplete sentence. It is missing a subject, a verb, or a main clause. To correct a fragment, add the missing part or join it to another sentence. Review the following fragments and possible corrections.

	FRAGMENTS	POSSIBLE CORRECTIONS
no subject	Pay for prisons.	**Add a subject:** **Taxpayers** pay for prisons.
no verb	First, the crime rate.	**Add a verb:** First, the crime rate **is dropping**.
no main clause	Because* he was hungry.	**Add a main clause:** **He stole food** because he was hungry.

* A subordinator such as *because* introduces a secondary idea. Make sure that your sentence also has a primary idea.

Run-on Sentences

A **run-on sentence** occurs when two complete ideas are joined incorrectly with a comma. Review the following run-on and possible corrections.

RUN-ON SENTENCE	POSSIBLE CORRECTIONS
Jeremy left prison, he found a job.	**Add a coordinator:** Jeremy left prison, **and** he found a job.
	Add a subordinator: **After** Jeremy left prison, he found a job.
	Add a semicolon: Jeremy left prison; he found a job.
	Make two complete sentences: Jeremy left prison. **He** found a job.

Answers will vary for sentence corrections.

EXERCISE 6 FRAGMENTS AND RUN-ONS

Write *F* beside fragments and *RO* beside run-ons. Write *C* beside correct sentences. Then correct the incorrect sentences.

                 is

EXAMPLE: History ^ sometimes complicated.   F

                        some men took

1. On April 6, 1909, ^ a trip across many miles of ice.   F

2. Who was the first person to reach the North Pole?   C

                           but

3. Robert Peary said he was the first, ^ he didn't tell the whole truth.   RO

He bent the truth, b

4. ^ Because five men were with him.   F

5. Peary's African American assistant was also at the North Pole.   C

There were f

6. ^ Four Inuit men, too.   F

7. Peary lost several toes during his northern journeys.   C

                            ;

8. Many history books mention Peary, ^ they don't mention the others.   RO

                     and

9. Peary wanted to be famous, ^ he succeeded.   RO

He's famous e

10. ^ Especially in Canada, where many history books detail his exploits.   F

EXERCISE 7 PUNCTUATION

Add five missing punctuation marks to each paragraph, for a total of twenty. When necessary, add a period (.), comma (,), colon (:), semicolon (;), or apostrophe ('). If necessary, review the information about punctuation on pages 122 and 123.

                        isn't

EXAMPLE: Starting a business ~~isnt~~ a simple process.

1. In 2001, Mr. Charlie Todd arrived in New York. After he arrived, he couldn't find acting work. Todd, an enterprising man, decided to stage his own comedy scenes.

2. With some friends, Todd used skill, creativity, and humour to develop his first public scene. The three friends bought the following supplies: a camera, grey pants, and a shark-head costume. As a joke, the "shark" pretended to attack students on a campus, but the prank wasn't very successful.   ➜

UNIT 11 | **Sentences and Punctuation** | 129

© ERPI • REPRODUCTION PROHIBITED

3. In 2002, they decided to have a "No Pants" event; it would occur on New York's subway. At 12:30 in the afternoon, seven people, including Todd, entered subway cars wearing only boxer shorts.

4. At first, the transit riders ignored the men with no pants. Then people's reactions changed; they started to laugh. Some subway riders' shocked reactions were hilarious. The entire episode, which was videotaped, ended up on YouTube.

TIP

Capitalization

Capitalize the names of specific places and titles. If you do not mention a specific name, no capitals are necessary.

There is a busy <u>street</u> near my home. It is called **P**eel **S**treet.

Ellis lives near a <u>river</u>. His house is near the **T**hames **R**iver.

EXERCISE 8 CAPITALIZATION

Add twenty-five missing capital letters. You can review the capitalization rules on page 124.

1. Flash mobs were invented by mr. Bill Wasik. In 2008, the first International Pillow fight day occurred on march 22. According to a *Wall street journal* reporter, people from around the world participated. Since then, there have been massive pillow fights every year. For example, last year, the special day was in the spring. On saturday, april 2, people in Amsterdam gathered in dam square to hit each other with pillows.

2. Many americans, australians, and canadians also joined in last year. In Austin, Texas, the pillow fight was at 7000 ardath street. In Toronto, the pillow fight wasn't near lake Ontario. Instead, it was on yonge street. People of all religions participated. There were christians, buddhists, and muslims at the events. Last year, there was an article in the *San Francisco examiner* called, "The evolution of flash mobs." It explains some of the benefits of flash mobs.

QUOTATION MARKS

In quotations, put a comma after an opening phrase. Put a colon after an opening sentence.

Comma: She said, "The riot was frightening."

Colon: She was very upset: "The riot was frightening."

When you place a phrase at the end of a quotation, end the quotation with a comma instead of a period.

"They were violent thugs," said the shop owner.

TIP

Inside Quotations

When one quotation is inside another quotation, use single quotation marks.

The journalist wrote, "People in the riot shouted, 'We are the 99 percent.'"

EXERCISE 9 QUOTATIONS

In the next sentences, the quotation is in bold. Punctuate each quotation, and add capital letters when necessary.

EXAMPLE: The interviewer asked, **"Why are you doing this?"**

1. In an interview with the CBC, Camilla said, **"The riot was enjoyable."**

2. The journalist replied, **"You destroyed property."**

3. Camilla declared, **"Everybody was rioting. I was not alone."**

4. The rioter was not sorry for her actions: **"You can't blame me. I was following the crowd."**

5. **"Some store owners lost everything,"** the journalist responded.

6. Camilla looked directly at the journalist: **"Nobody could stop the riot."**

COMMON PUNCTUATION ERRORS

Do not separate the subject and verb with a comma.

The young man~~,~~ was excited about his business.

Don't use apostrophes before the final –s of a verb or a plural noun.

     wants   **towns**

Moira ~~want's~~ to visit several ~~town's~~.

In negative contractions, don't put the apostrophe before the –nt.
The apostrophe replaces the missing –o in *not*.

     doesn't

She ~~does'nt~~ have free time.

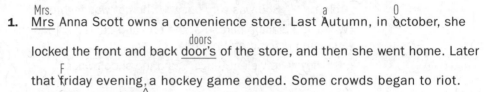

EXERCISE 10 · IDENTIFY ERRORS

Correct fifteen errors in capitalization or punctuation. You may need to add or remove punctuation marks and capital letters.

                               J
EXAMPLE: The riot began in july.

   Mrs.

1. <u>Mrs</u> Anna Scott owns a convenience store. Last Autumn, in october, she
                                                 a   O

                                  doors
   locked the front and back <u>door's</u> of the store, and then she went home. Later
                  F

   that friday evening, a hockey game ended. Some crowds began to riot.

2. Someone threw a brick through Anna Browns store window. A spectator

   said "Let's rob that store." The thieves stole the following, pants,
                                                      didn't

   shirts, and jackets. Some hockey fans were honest and <u>did'nt</u> steal.

   Instead, they took cellphone videos of the thieves.
                     G   remove comma

3. Several german tourists, were shocked at the actions of the crowd.
            A

   Last april, one of the visiting tourists wrote a book about riots called
                             I

   Collective insanity.

↺ UNIT Review

<table>
<tr><td>As you go over the answers to question 1 in the Unit Review, ask students to explain why each sentence is incorrect.</td><td>Answer the following questions. If you don't know an answer, go back and review the appropriate section.</td></tr>
</table>

1. Identify the error in each sentence. Then write a rule about each error.

   a) First, the funniest movie.   <u>fragment</u>

       Rule: <u>A sentence must have a subject and verb and express a complete idea.</u>

   b) She made a movie who was very successful.   <u>that</u>

       Rule: <u>Use *who* to give information about people only.</u>

   c) The movie was a love story, it was about a wedding.   <u>run-on</u>

       Rule: <u>You can't join two complete ideas with a comma.</u>

   d) It was about a girl who's wedding was complicated.   <u>whose</u>

       Rule: <u>*Who's* is the contracted form of *who is*.</u>

   e) Although many people came to the wedding.   <u>fragment</u>

       Rule: <u>Add this type of fragment to another sentence.</u>

2. Add ten missing punctuation marks and/or capital letters to the following sentences.

a) Mr.Carubba closes his store every winter during the month of january.
      ^   J

b) The crime occurred on main street on a friday.
                             M   S   F

c) The thief, who entered through a window, stole the following items:rings,
                                          ^   ^
watches, and necklaces.

d) In an article called "Crime rates rise," a reporter said, "The criminal
                                  R   R   ^
stole $10,000 worth of items."

Need more practice?
Visit the Companion Website and try additional grammar exercises.

Final Review

You can use the Final Review as a test. There are ten answers each in Parts A, B, and C, for a total of thirty points. You can also find additional practice exercises and testing material on the Companion Website.

Answers may vary.

PART A

Correct the errors in the sentences below. Write *C* next to correct sentences.

                                  that
    EXAMPLE: Medical science is a subject ~~who~~ I adore.

                      and some
1. Some stories are true, <u>some</u> are interesting legends.

          there are
2. For example, many urban myths.

                  stories because
3. People believe the <u>stories. Because</u> they usually happened to "a friend of a friend."

             that
4. In one story, a worm <u>who</u> is inside a man's ear eats his brain.

                 reptiles, especially
5. Most people are afraid of <u>reptiles. Especially</u> snakes and alligators.

6. Another story is about alligators that live in public sewer systems. C

           which
7. One story, <u>wich</u> I enjoyed a lot, is about a woman who buys a chihuahua.

          that
8. She discovers <u>than</u> her little dog is actually a rat!

         popular, although
9. Rats are not <u>popular. Although</u> I actually like them.

         purpose. They
10. The stories have a <u>purpose, they</u> are about collective fear.

PART B

Underline the correct word in parentheses.

11. Our nation has a lot of homeless people. Our city, (<u>which</u> / who) has very cold winters, needs to take action. For example, Mark Webb, (<u>who's</u> / whose / who) just twenty-five years old, has been homeless for six years. Like many youths (<u>who</u> / which) live on the streets, Webb comes from a violent family. He loves his parents; (although / <u>however</u>), he can't live with them. (<u>Although</u> / However) his mother is attentive, his father is an alcoholic. Webb, (who's / <u>whose</u> / who) sleeping bag is wet, needs a place to live.

12. Many homeless youths need protection; (<u>however</u>, although), the government does not provide enough resources. Youths (whose / <u>who</u> / who's) can't return home end up on the streets. This is a problem (than / <u>that</u> / who) will not go away. The economy is getting worse, (<u>but</u> / so / or) the government is not taking action.

PART C

Add ten missing punctuation marks and capital letters to the following paragraphs.

13. "Occupy" demonstrations began in 2011. On ̇O̶ctober 15, Canada's first protest occurred in Vancouver on ̶Hornby ̶Street, which is across the street from the Vancouver ̶Art Gallery. About eighty people carried signs, and many set up tents. They didn't̶ didnt seem very happy. One sign said, ̂ "Justice for the 99 percent."

14. A man shouted at the crowd:̂ "Fight for your rights!" The protesters had the following complaints:̂ bank bonuses are too high, the middle class is shrinking, and jobs are scarce. Mrs. Wright, who was the oldest person there, said that the protesters'̶ protesters complaints were legitimate.

You can ask students to complete the final review and then detach this page. In the students' books, pages are perforated.

SPEAKING AND WRITING

"Dear Minister: ..."

Working with a partner, write a letter to a government minister. Ask the minister to take action regarding the homeless. Brainstorm some specific actions that governments can take. Include the names of some streets where there are homeless people.

Students can do the writing exercise on a separate sheet of paper. Once they have finished, ask them to exchange sheets with another team and peer edit for correct sentence structure, capitalization, and punctuation.

Word Form

Preview

WHAT IS THE PASSIVE VOICE?

When the subject does not do the action, the verb is passive.

Active: Italian workers **made** my leather shoes.
Passive: My shoes **were made** in Italy (by Italian workers).
(The shoes do not do the action.)

USE PASSIVE VERB FORMS

Practise using the passive form in different verb tenses. Put a form of the verb *to be* in the space provided.

EXAMPLE: Simple present: New food products <u>are</u> produced every year.

Tense or Modal	Passive Verb Form
1. Simple present	A new invention _____is_____ made every day.
2. Simple present	Several inventions _____are_____ patented every week.
3. Simple past	That cellphone _____was_____ developed many years ago.
4. Future	The new cellphone model _____will be_____ sold next year.
5. Present perfect	More than thirty inventions _____have been_____ patented by Marcus Roo.
6. Modal auxiliary "can"	A cellphone _____can be_____ used anywhere.

Passive Voice: Forms and Usage

Look carefully at the following two sentences. Notice the differences between the **active** and the **passive** voice.

Ben **sold** the car.   This is **active** because the subject (*Ben*) did the action.

The car **was sold**.   This is **passive** because the subject (*the car*) was affected by the action. The subject did not do the action.

To form the passive voice, use the verb *be* + the past participle.

ACTIVE AND PASSIVE FORMS

VERB TENSES AND MODALS	ACTIVE (The subject is acting.)	PASSIVE (The subject receives the action.) be + past participle
Simple present	They make shoes.	Shoes **are made** by them.
Present progressive	are making	**are being made**
Simple past	made	**were made**
Present perfect	have made	**have been made**
Future	will make	**will be made**
can	can make	**can be made**
could	could make	**could be made**
should	should make	**should be made**
would	would make	**would be made**
must	must make	**must be made**

To be
Use the past participle after **to be**.

> EXAMPLE: Children need <u>to be</u> **loved**.

Gerunds and Infinitives: Forms and Usage

GERUNDS AS SUBJECTS
Usually, the subject of a sentence is a noun. A **gerund** is an "ing" verb that functions as a noun.

> **Running** is a good cardio workout.

GERUNDS AND INFINITIVES
When a verb appears after another verb, use the **infinitive form** most of the time. The **infinitive** consists of *to* + the base form of the verb.

> **Infinitive:** I <u>need</u> **to leave**.   People <u>want</u> **to have** a good life.

Sometimes, the second verb is a **gerund**, or "ing" verb.

> **Gerund:**   Shakira <u>enjoys</u> **singing**.   She <u>finished</u> **signing** autographs.

Practice

Ask students to identify passive and active verbs in Exercise 1. They can also practise identifying passive verbs by doing exercises on the Companion Website.

EXERCISE 1 CHOOSING ACTIVE OR PASSIVE VERBS

Underline the appropriate verb forms below. Then write *P* (for "passive") or *A* (for "active") in the blanks.

> EXAMPLE: The house (built / <u>was built</u>) __P__ in 1951.

1. The first North American suburb (created / <u>was created</u>) __P__ by William Levitt. At the time, returning World War II soldiers (<u>needed</u> / were needed) __A__ affordable housing.

Housing (offered / <u>was offered</u>) ___P___ to soldiers and their families by Canadian and American governments. Soldiers (supposed / <u>were supposed</u>) ___P___ to apply for the housing.

2. The first suburb—Levittown—was not an attractive place. Houses (designed / <u>were designed</u>) ___P___ with identical shapes. They (painted / <u>were painted</u>) ___P___ in five different colours. Sometimes, when residents (<u>arrived</u> / were arrived) ___A___ home, they could not find their houses.

3. These days, some communities (have built / <u>have been built</u>) ___P___ with "New Urbanism" principles. For example, in my city, a construction company (<u>will build</u> / will be built) ___A___ houses that use "green" energy. People (<u>won't pay</u> / won't be paid) ___A___ electricity bills. Also, cars (won't need / <u>won't be needed</u>) ___P___ by the new owners. Stores and public transportation (will construct / <u>will be constructed</u>) ___P___ a short distance from homes. Perhaps one day, I (<u>will buy</u> / will be bought) ___A___ an energy-efficient home.

THE BASE FORM VERSUS THE PAST PARTICIPLE

Use the past participle (e.g., *moved, broken, seen*)

- of passive verbs and verbs that follow *to be*;
   The movie <u>was</u> **made** in 2005. It needs <u>to be</u> **marketed**.

- of verbs that follow *have, has,* or *had* in the perfect tenses.
   I <u>have</u> **seen** many films. My sister <u>has</u> never **bought** a television.

Use the base form (e.g., *go, eat, talk*)

- of verbs that follow the single word *to* in infinitive forms;
   She wanted <u>to</u> **move** to a suburb.

- of verbs that follow *do, does,* or *did* in question and negative forms.
   <u>Did</u> he **study** yesterday? He <u>didn't</u> **go** to work.

EXERCISE 2 CORRECTING WORD-FORM ERRORS

Underline and correct word-form errors.

EXAMPLE: The bear was <u>film</u> by a homeowner.
     filmed

1. Many problems are <u>cause</u> by urban sprawl.
     caused

2. For instance, last year, the majority of people in my neighbourhood didn't <u>used</u> public transportation.
     use

3. Wildlife can also be also <u>affect</u> by urban sprawl.
     affected   →

4. Many species, such as deer and foxes, have been <u>force</u> *(forced)* to leave urban areas.

5. Last year, in Vancouver, a bear did not <u>abandoned</u> *(abandon)* its traditional habitat.

6. Carol Wang needed to <u>called</u> *(call)* wildlife officials.

7. A sleeping black bear was <u>discover</u> *(discovered)* in her backyard.

8. In recent years, many people have <u>saw</u> *(seen)* falcons on city rooftops.

9. Skunks have been <u>find</u> *(found)* under people's porches.

10. In some towns, deer are <u>consider</u> *(considered)* pests because they destroy gardens.

11. Last week, a raccoon was <u>chase</u> *(chased)* off my street by an angry neighbour.

12. Since 2000, animal-control officers have <u>remove</u> *(removed)* about two hundred wild animals from our area.

CHOOSING –*ING* OR –*ED*

Some adjectives look like verbs because they end in **–*ing*** or **–*ed***.

When an adjective ends in –*ed*, it describes the person or animal's expression or feeling.

The **interested** audience listened to the presentation.

When an adjective ends in –*ing*, it describes a quality of the person or thing.

The **interesting** speaker described his experiences in Beijing.

TIP

Considered

Never write "considerated." It is not a word! Instead, use *considered*. The adjective *considerate* means "thoughtful; kind."

                   considered
Montreal is ~~considerated~~ a great city.   Adrianna is a **considerate** host.

EXERCISE 3 CHOOSING –*ING* OR –*ED*

Underline the correct form of the verbs in parentheses.

    EXAMPLE: Physics can be a very (confused / <u>confusing</u>) subject for some people.

1. In June 2011, seventeen-year-old Nathan Kotylak was a (respecting / <u>respected</u>) polo player, and he was (considering / considerate / <u>considered</u>) an important member of Canada's junior water-polo team. But that month, he made a

(<u>surprising</u> / surprised) decision. After Vancouver lost the Stanley Cup playoffs, Nathan joined a (<u>rioting</u> / rioted) mob. He was (<u>photographed</u> / photographing) holding a burning rag near a police car.

2. Two days later, his face, name, address, and phone number were on Facebook and "name and shame" websites. His family was (<u>threatened</u> / threatening) by angry citizens. His (frightening / <u>frightened</u>) family moved to another place. His parents were (disturbing / <u>disturbed</u>) by the public's response. But they were also angry with Nathan for his (<u>disappointing</u> / disappointed) conduct.

3. Nathan Kotylak decided to rebuild his (<u>damaged</u> / damaging) reputation. In a statement to the media, he apologized for his (<u>shocking</u> / shocked) actions.

GERUNDS AS SUBJECTS

When the subject of a sentence is an action, the action verb can be transformed into a noun by adding *–ing*. The "ing" verb is called a **gerund**.

Exercising is good for the health.

EXERCISE 4 GERUNDS AS SUBJECTS

PART A

Turn each verb into a gerund subject.

EXAMPLE: (find) _____Finding_____ a job is difficult.

1. (sing) _____Singing_____ is good for the health.

2. (help) _____Helping_____ others is very satisfying.

3. (smoke) _____Smoking_____ is very bad for the lungs.

4. (make) _____Making_____ jokes about other people is cruel.

PART B

Underline and correct four subject errors.

EXAMPLE: <u>Walk</u> every day is good exercise. *(Walking)*

5. <u>Travel</u> is a good way to learn about the world. We discover new beliefs *(Travelling)* and cuisines. Also, <u>learn</u> another language helps us feel connected *(learning)* with others. Basically, <u>study</u> the ways that other people live makes *(studying)* us better global citizens. People should learn about the world. <u>Be</u> *(Being)* a global citizen is great.

GERUNDS AFTER VERBS

When a verb appears after another verb, **use the infinitive form most of the time**. But remember that sometimes the second verb is a **gerund**, or "ing" verb.

Infinitive: He <u>likes</u> **to eat**. She <u>wants</u> **to drive**. He <u>hopes</u> **to graduate**.
Gerund: He <u>enjoys</u> **eating**. She <u>finished</u> **driving**.

Some Common Verbs Followed by Gerunds

avoid	dislike	finish	miss	quit
deny	enjoy	keep	practise	regret

Some Common Verbs Followed by Gerunds or Infinitives

Some common verbs can be followed by either gerunds or infinitives. Both forms have the same meaning.

begin	continue	like	love	start

Infinitive: She <u>began</u> **to eat**.
Gerund: She <u>began</u> **eating**.

Stop and *Used to*

Some verbs can be followed by either a gerund or an infinitive, but there is a difference in meaning depending on the form you use.

FORM	MEANING	EXAMPLE
stop + infinitive	to stop an activity in order to do something	He <u>stops</u> **to buy** gas every Sunday.
stop + gerund	to stop doing something permanently	I <u>stopped</u> **buying** cigarettes five years ago.
used to + infinitive	to express a past habit or situation	Jeff <u>used</u> **to live** alone.
be used to + gerund	to be accustomed to something	Jeff <u>is used to</u> **living** alone.

TIP

Gerund or Progressive Verb Form?

Do not confuse **gerunds** with **progressive verb forms**. Compare a gerund and a progressive verb:

Gerund: Xavier <u>finished</u> **studying**.
(After *finish*, use a gerund.)

Progressive verb: Xavier **is studying** now.
(He is in the process of doing something.)

EXERCISE 5 GERUNDS AND INFINITIVES

Underline the correct form of the verbs in parentheses.

1. When I was a teenager, I (<u>used to smoke</u> / used to smoking). Like many adolescents, I wanted (<u>to look</u> / looking) cool. At first, I didn't enjoy (to puff / <u>puffing</u>) on a cigarette. It made my throat hurt. But I soon became (used to smoke / <u>used to smoking</u>). I intended (fitting / <u>to fit</u>) in with my friends.

2. About five years later, I got sick. I couldn't stop (to cough / <u>coughing</u>). I knew that I had (<u>to do</u> / doing) something about my cigarette habit, but I was addicted. Sometimes, I would finish (to smoke / <u>smoking</u>) a cigarette, and I would promise myself that it would be the last one. But whenever I was near a convenience store, I would stop (buying / <u>to buy</u>) cigarettes, and then I would smoke them. I kept (<u>smoking</u> / to smoke) off and on for several more years.

3. One day, my doctor told me that I really needed (quitting / <u>to quit</u>). I had developed a growth in my throat. I was so scared that I decided (<u>to take</u> / taking) action right away. That night, I quit (to smoke / <u>smoking</u>). Nowadays, I (used to live / <u>am used to living</u>) a smoke-free life. Sometimes I miss (to smoke / <u>smoking</u>), but most days I don't think about it. I hope (<u>to have</u> / having) a long and healthy life!

↩ UNIT Review

Answer the following questions. If you don't know an answer, go back and review the appropriate section.

1. Identify the underlined verbs as active (*A*) or passive (*P*).

   a) The meeting <u>was cancelled</u>.   P

   b) The president <u>cancelled</u> the meeting   A

   c) Coffee <u>is being served</u> by the assistant.   P

   d) The assistant <u>is serving</u> the coffee.   A

2. Underline and correct the word-form error in each of the next sentences.

   a) Sara is <u>exciting</u> about music.   excited

   b) <u>Write</u> songs is her passion.   Writing

   c) She wants to be <u>accept</u> into the music program.   accepted

   d) The college is <u>admire</u> because it has great music teachers.   admired

   e) Sara has <u>send</u> her application form three times.   sent

   f) She won't stop <u>to try</u> until she is accepted.   trying

© ERPI • REPRODUCTION PROHIBITED

Need more practice?
Visit the Companion Website and try additional grammar exercises.

UNIT 12 | **Word Form** | 141

Final Review

You can use the Final Review as a test. There are ten answers in Part A and fifteen answers in Part B for a total of twenty-five points. You can also find additional practice exercises and testing material on the Companion Website.

PART A

Underline and correct the word-form error in each sentence. Write *C* beside correct sentences.

EXAMPLE: The actress was <u>interview</u> by the journalist.   <u>interviewed</u>

1. In January 2009, in the locker room of a European spa, some women were <u>film</u> by a voyeur.   <u>filmed</u>

2. Over the years, many teachers have <u>complain</u> about students and cellphone cameras.   <u>complained</u>

3. In the past, nobody wanted to <u>discussed</u> the issue.   <u>discuss</u>

4. In 2011, a schoolteacher's anger was <u>record</u> by a student.   <u>recorded</u>

5. The teacher said, "I was <u>humiliate</u> by that student!"   <u>humiliated</u>

6. In the past, some people didn't <u>believed</u> that cellphone cameras were a problem.   <u>believe</u>

7. These days, many citizens have <u>took</u> videos of others' bad actions and posted the videos on YouTube.   <u>taken</u>

8. For example, in 2010, a cat was put in a garbage bin by an old woman.   <u>C</u>

9. Mary Bale was publicly <u>shame</u> when the video was posted on YouTube.   <u>shamed</u>

10. In 2010, many animal lovers wanted Bale to be <u>arrest</u>.   <u>arrested</u>

PART B

Underline the correct words in parentheses.

If you asked students to skip the "Gerunds" section in this unit, then they should stop after question 12 in Part B. Their "quiz" would then have fifteen points instead of twenty-five points.

11. A few years ago, the "cat-bin lady" video appeared on YouTube, and it became a huge sensation. Viewers watched Mary Bale's (<u>surprising</u> / surprised) action as she calmly picked up a cat and dropped it into a huge garbage bin. She didn't (<u>realize</u> / realized) that a security camera was filming her.

12. A few days later, someone recognized Bale from the YouTube video, and her name was (release / <u>released</u> / releasing) to the public. When Bale protested that "it was just a cat," animal lovers were (enrage / <u>enraged</u>). Instantly, she received death threats. She was even (chase / <u>chased</u> / chasing) by the paparazzi!

13. Bale definitely wasn't (<u>used to receiving</u> / used to receive) so much attention. (Have / <u>Having</u>) a lot of enemies is not enjoyable. She stopped (to appear / <u>appearing</u>) in public and secluded herself at home. At one point, she decided (<u>to move</u> / moving) to another house because she didn't (<u>feel</u> / felt) safe in her own home.

14. (Be / <u>Being</u> / Is) an Internet celebrity was horrible for Mary Bale. She wanted people (<u>to forget</u> / forgetting) about her. She didn't enjoy (to be / <u>being</u>) in the public eye.

15. If we stop (<u>to think</u> / thinking) about the abundance of cameras everywhere, it is worrisome. We could be (film / <u>filmed</u>) at any time!

SPEAKING AND WRITING

Students can do the writing exercise on a separate sheet of paper.

Edit a Letter

In the letter below, the writer overuses the passive voice. The letter would be clearer if the writer had used the active voice. With a partner, underline the passive verbs, and then rewrite the letter using the active voice.

Your letter has been received by us. You will be contacted by a sales representative soon. Your television will be repaired by our technician, and your account.will be credited. If you have any further questions, we can be contacted during working hours.

EXAMPLE: We have received your letter.

_____

_____

_____

_____

_____

_____

_____

_____

_____

_____

_____

_____

_____

_____

_____

Editing Practice and Tense Review

Note that editing symbols are added to exercises 1 to 3 so that students can practise editing using those symbols.

Practise editing student writing. The following exercises contain a variety of errors.

EXERCISE 1 EDITING

Correct the twenty errors in this student paragraph, not including the example. An editing symbol appears above each error. To understand the meaning of each symbol, look at the "Guide for Correcting Writing Errors" on the inside back cover of this book.

        English   another
          C   ◯

Today, in my <u>english</u> class, I had a short conversation with <u>an other</u> student. Raul is

    interesting   is   lives
    SP   WC   SV

a very <u>interresting</u> person. He <u>has</u> eighteen years old, and he <u>live</u> near the college.

    works   weekend   store   learning
    SV   PL   ◯   WF

He <u>work</u> every <u>weekends</u> at a grocery ʌ. According to Raul, <u>learn</u> a second language

                 increases   person's
                  SV   P

is important because it <u>increase</u> a <u>persons</u> chance to find a good job. In the past,

      travelled   there are/were
      VT   WC

Raul <u>was travelling</u> to Spain and Costa Rica. He said that <u>it have</u> many beautiful

                 country   much   doesn't
                 SP   X   SV

beaches in Costa Rica, but the <u>contry</u> was also too <u>~~much~~</u> dangerous. He <u>don't</u> plan

                      like   S
                      WF   C

to return to Costa Rica. However, he would <u>likes</u> to return to Spain. He speaks <u>spanish</u>

                                              '
                                            P

well and can communicate with the citizens. He said<u>:</u> "I love Barcelona. It is the most

                         "
                                               J
                       P   C

beautiful city in the world". Next summer, during the month of <u>july</u>, he will travel again.

EXERCISE 2 EDITING

Correct twenty-five errors in the student paragraphs, not including the example.
An editing symbol appears above each error. To understand the meaning of each
symbol, look at the "Guide for Correcting Writing Errors" on the inside back cover
of this book.

              the   day   for
              ◯   PL   WC

1. Many students go on ⌃Internet every <u>days</u>. In fact, <u>since</u> a couple of years,

                         have been   people
                           VT   SP

online social networking and YouTube <u>are</u> really popular. Some <u>persons</u> think

that they need to be online constantly. However, online sites can have serious

disadvantages.

                         post
                         VT

2. First, many people <u>are posting</u> messages daily, and they share too much

    information   themselves   their   which
      PL   SP   WF   SP
<u>informations</u> about <u>theirselves</u>. They post photos of <u>theirs</u> parties, <u>wich</u> can

                                                see
                                              WF
cause problems later. Maybe a boss or a grandmother will <u>seeing</u> the photos.

                                         lives   example
                                       SP   SP
Also, some students write too many details about their <u>lifes</u> online. For <u>exemple</u>,

                she   always discusses   private
            DS   VT   PL
my friend <u>she</u> <u>is always discussing</u> her feelings, and she provides <u>privates</u> details

                                                 to
                                              ◯
about her day on a social-networking site. I don't need ⌃see her or speak with

      her, because
         F
her<u>. Because</u> I can just read her posts.

                                                      forget
                                                  VT

3. Also, computer games, videos, and blogs can make people <u>forgot</u> the real people

                                  . They
                                  RO
in their lives. They hide in a "cyber" world<u>, they</u> don't interact with others. For

                                   hundred
                                   PL
example, Hal Niedzviecki invited his seven <u>hundreds</u> Facebook friends to a

party. Fifteen people responded that they would come, but only one person

weren't
SV

came. Niedzviecki realized that his online friends <u>wasn't</u> true friends.

It's
P
4. <u>Its</u> a good idea to take a break from the Internet. How will <u>live most people</u> in

most people live
WO

future
SP
the <u>futur</u> ? One of the best <u>decision</u> anyone can make is to live a real life and

decisions
PL

not a cyber life.

EXERCISE 3 EDITING

Underline and correct twenty errors in this student text. An editing symbol appears above each error. To understand the meaning of each symbol, look at the "Guide for Correcting Writing Errors" on the inside back cover of this book.

absolutely different things
WO
1. High school and college are two <u>things absolutely different</u>. High school has

some advantages and disadvantages. In high school, students are very

supervised
WF
<u>supervise</u>. They can't do what they want. If they miss a <u>cours</u>, they will have

course
SP

hand
WC
a detention or some additional assignments. On the other <u>side</u>, high-school

are
SV
teachers <u>is</u> less severe. If a student <u>miss</u> an exam for no reason, or if he just

misses
SV

doesn't
SV
<u>don't</u> want to go <u>at</u> school, he will <u>has</u> a chance to do the exam later. Teachers

to
WC

have
WF

homework
PL
assign easy <u>homeworks</u>. Also, in high school, <u>it have</u> many social workers and

there are
WC

help
SV
psychologists who <u>helps</u> students.

students'
P
2. In college, <u>students</u> schedules are more flexible, but they have more work

that
WC
to do. They have to read books <u>who</u> are difficult. Most teachers don't give

a second chance if a student skips an exam. In college, everyone must ~~to~~ [X, to] deal

with a lot of work. But college makes students feeling [feel, WF] more independent.

Students work ~~more~~ [X, more] harder, they have to act more mature. Although, [and, RO] [P,] college

is more difficult then [than, WC] high school, it is also more interesting.

EXERCISE 4 FAULTY PRONOUN SHIFTS

Read this selection from a student essay. Underline and correct six faulty pronoun shifts, not including the example.

Many people follow fashion trends, but <u>your</u> [their] decisions can have financial

consequences. It costs a lot to be in style. When people go to the mall, <u>we</u> [they] may

buy designer clothing because <u>we</u> [they] want to be "in." People pay a lot for the clothes,

so <u>you</u> [they] can have large debts. Consumers also go to hair salons to have the latest

hairstyles. But cutting and colouring hair can cost about $100, so <u>you</u> [they] spend a lot.

For example, my friend Amelie spends all of her money on fashion. She never has

extra money. Maybe she should realize that <u>your</u> [her] fashion choices are not important.

If her clothes are clean, then people will appreciate <u>us</u> [her].

Discuss faulty pronoun and tense shifts. Remind students about the importance of tense and pronoun consistency.

TIP

Would and *Could*

When you tell a story about a past event, remember to use *would* instead of *will*, and *could* instead of *can*.

              would   **could**

In the 1990s, boys ~~will~~ wear extra-large pants. Without a belt, their pants ~~can~~ fall down.

EXERCISE 5 FAULTY TENSE SHIFTS

Underline and correct six faulty tense shifts, not including the example.

    Tattoos are very popular. Every day, people <u>went</u> [go] to tattoo parlours and <u>received</u> [receive]

permanent marks on their bodies. For example, five years ago, when I was fourteen,

I really wanted a tattoo. My parents said that they <u>won't</u> [wouldn't] pay for it. I had some birthday

money, so I <u>can</u> [could] pay for it myself. I went to a tattoo parlour, and I got a tattoo on my

shoulder. I wanted to have a tattoo of my favourite singer's face. When my parents

saw my tattoo, they said that I <u>will</u> [would] regret my actions. I <u>don't</u> [didn't] believe them. But

these days, I realize that they were right. I hate my tattoo. The colour is fading to

green, and it <u>was</u> [is] ugly. Also, I don't like the singer anymore, so I don't want to have

the image of his face on my body. In the future, I will pay to remove the tattoo with

a laser.

EXERCISE 6 "HOW" QUESTIONS

Add the missing word to each question. Choose from the following:

    far   long   many   much   often   old

    EXAMPLE: How _much_ is that coat? Is it $15?

1. How _____old_____ are you? Are you sixteen years old?

2. How _____often_____ do you go to movie theatres? Do you go once a month?

3. How _____long_____ is the movie: two or three hours?

4. How _____many_____ people are in the lineup? Are there a lot of people?

5. How _____far_____ is Boston? Is it more than 200 kilometres from here?

6. How _____old_____ was Reena when she moved away? Was she twenty years old?

7. How _____long_____ have you been in college? Have you been here for one or two years?

8. How _____much_____ is that house? Does it cost more than $200,000?

EXERCISE 7 QUESTIONS

Students wrote questions for Mark Zuckerberg, the co-inventor of Facebook. Correct the error in each sentence.

              do
EXAMPLE: Where ᵧou live?

         were
1. In the past, was your parents rich?

         be   be
2. In the future, what will be your greatest legacy?

         do
3. What did you before you invented Facebook?

       did you start
4. When you started your company?

      are you
5. Where you are living now?

      long
6. How many times have you been living in California, and do you like it there?

       do
7. Every day, what you do in your spare time?

     have you known
8. How long do you know your girlfriend?

     will you
9. In the future, you will start another company?

EXERCISE 8 TEN KEY RULES

In this exercise, errors represent ten major grammar problems. Each error is in bold. Correct the error. Then write a rule for each correction.

        decisions
1. One of my best **decision** was to return to college.

    Rule: ___Use a plural noun after "one of."___

    See Unit 1, page 4, for more information about plurals.

        homework   information
2. We do a lot of **homeworks**. Our books have a lot of **informations**.

    Rule: ___Some nouns are "noncount" and have no plural form.___

    See Unit 1, page 3, for more information about noncount nouns.

Have students do Exercise 8 in teams. You can make this a timed competition.

3.   *There are*

     They have a lot of reasons why people make YouTube videos. **It have** good   *There are*

     reasons and bad reasons.

     Rule: Use *there is/there are* to show that something exists.

     See Unit 2, page 17, for more information about *there is* and *there are*.

4.   *needs*   *wants*

     Everyone **need** clear goals. For example, my friend **want** to be a singer.

     Rule: In the present, add *–s* or *–es* to verbs that follow third-person singular subjects.

     See Unit 2, page 15, for more information about subject-verb agreement.

5.   *visited*   *stayed*

     When I was young, I **was visiting** Florida every year. Each time, I **was staying** at

     my aunt's house.

     Rule: Do not use the past progressive unless a past action was in progress at a particular past time.

     See Unit 3, page 31, for more information about the past tenses.

6.   *have been*   *have you been*

     Since September, I **am** a student. How long **are you** a student at this college?

     Rule: Use the present perfect when an action began in the past and continues to the present.

     See Unit 5, page 54, for more information about the present perfect tense.

7.   *to*   *to*

     Last summer, I went **in** Europe with my family. Each summer, we go **at** a new place.

     Rule: Put *to* after *go.*

     See Unit 8, page 93, for more information about prepositions.

8.   *Other*   *different*

     Others people have **differents** values. They don't have the same beliefs as

     their

     theirs parents.

     Rule: Adjectives are never plural.

     See Unit 9, page 105, for more information about adjectives.

9.   *It's*   *and*

     People love to **travel, it's** a passion for them. They visit other **countries, they**

     learn many things.

     Rule: Do not join two complete ideas with a comma.

     See Unit 11, page 128, for more information about sentence errors.

10.   *write*   *try*

     Chandra didn't **wrote** the report. Everyone should **tried** to be honest.

     Rule: Use the base form of the verb after *did, can, could, should,* etc.

     See Unit 12, page 137 for more information about word form.

Parts of Speech

PART OF SPEECH	DEFINITION	EXAMPLES
adjective	▪ adds information about the noun	small, hot, beautiful, green
adverb	▪ adds information about the verb ▪ expresses time, place, and frequency	easily, nicely, quickly, quietly sometimes, usually, often, never
conjunction	▪ connects two parts of a sentence – **coordinating:** connects two ideas of equal importance – **subordinating:** connects a subordinate (or secondary) idea to the main idea	 and, but, so, or, yet after, although, because, unless
determiner	▪ identifies or determines if the noun is specific or general	a, an, the, this, that, these, those, each, every, much, many, some
noun (common)	▪ a person, place, or thing	**singular:** woman, cat, person **plural:** women, cats, people
noun (proper)	▪ a specific person, place, or thing – Proper nouns are capitalized.	Jamaica, Dr. Reed, Samson, Lake Ontario, Golden Gate Bridge, Calgary
preposition	▪ shows a relationship between words (source, direction, location, etc.)	above, at, behind, below, for, from, of, to
pronoun	▪ replaces the noun	he, she, it, us, ours, themselves
verb	▪ expresses an action or state	talk, walk, think, drive

PRACTICE

Label each word with one of the following terms.

adjective	conjunction	noun	pronoun
adverb	determiner	preposition	verb

EXAMPLE: clear   <u>adjective</u>

1. himself   <u>pronoun</u>
2. but   <u>conjunction</u>
3. human   <u>noun</u>
4. deliver   <u>verb</u>
5. above   <u>preposition</u>
6. white   <u>adjective</u>
7. often   <u>adverb</u>

8. into   <u>preposition</u>
9. hers   <u>pronoun</u>
10. make   <u>verb</u>
11. these   <u>determiner</u>
12. peacefully   <u>adverb</u>
13. Mr. Roy   <u>noun</u>
14. the   <u>determiner</u>

Identify the Past Perfect Tense

Before you teach conditional sentences (Unit 10), you could ask students to do this page in pairs.

The past perfect tense indicates that one past action happened before another past action. It is formed with *had* + the past participle.

Last night, the robbers **had** already **left** when the police arrived at the bank.

distant past → past → present

The robbers **had left**.   The police arrived.

PRACTICE

Read the pairs of sentences and underline the past perfect tense. Then answer each question.

1. Melanie <u>had</u> already <u>left</u> the hotel when I arrived.
   Marco left the hotel when I arrived.
   Who did I pass when I opened the door at the hotel? ___Marco___

2. When the second robbery occurred, the police put Rex in jail.
   When the second robbery occurred, the police <u>had</u> just <u>put</u> Jimmy in jail.
   Who could not have committed the second robbery? ___Jimmy___

3. Rihanna ate when Jeff invited her to dinner.
   Amber <u>had</u> already <u>eaten</u> when Jeff invited her to dinner.
   Who was not hungry when Jeff invited her to dinner? ___Amber___

4. When Julie entered the swimming competition, she <u>had won</u> two medals.
   When Carmen entered the swimming competition, she won two medals.
   Who was a medal winner before she entered the swimming competition? ___Julie___

5. The sun <u>had risen</u> when Anna woke up.
   The sun rose when Enrique woke up.
   Who missed the sunrise? ___Anna___

6. I rented a movie. Jay <u>had</u> already <u>watched</u> it.
   I rented a movie. Sam watched it.
   Who enjoyed the movie with me? ___Sam___

To practise using the past perfect tense, visit the Companion Website. Try Exercise 9 in the "Mixed Tenses and Questions" unit.

Note: Past conditional forms require the past perfect tense. (See page 114 in Unit 10.)

Irregular Verb List

The following list has four columns:

The **base form** appears in dictionaries. Use the base form in the present tense after auxiliaries such as *do, did, does, can,* or *should,* and after *to* in infinitives.

> **EXAMPLE:** You didn't <u>help</u>.

Use the **simple past** form with the simple past tense. (See Unit 3.)

> **EXAMPLE:** We <u>bought</u> a ticket yesterday.

Use the **past participle** form in perfect and passive structures. (See Units 5 and 12).

> **EXAMPLE:** She <u>has been</u> to England three times.

In the **meaning** column, write definitions or translations of verbs that you don't understand.

BASE FORM	SIMPLE PAST	PAST PARTICIPLE	MEANING	BASE FORM	SIMPLE PAST	PAST PARTICIPLE	MEANING
be	was/were	been		drink	drank	drunk	
beat	beat	beat/beaten		drive	drove	driven	
become	became	become		eat	ate	eaten	
begin	began	begun		fall	fell	fallen	
bend	bent	bent		feed	fed	fed	
bet	bet	bet		feel	felt	felt	
bite	bit	bitten		fight	fought	fought	
bleed	bled	bled		find	found	found	
blow	blew	blown		fit	fit	fit	
break	broke	broken		fly	flew	flown	
bring	brought	brought		forbid	forbade	forbidden	
build	built	built		forget	forgot	forgotten	
buy	bought	bought		forgive	forgave	forgiven	
catch	caught	caught		freeze	froze	frozen	
choose	chose	chosen		get	got	got/gotten	
come	came	come		give	gave	given	
cost	cost	cost		go	went	gone	
cut	cut	cut		grow	grew	grown	
deal	dealt	dealt		hang[1]	hung	hung	
dig	dug	dug		have	had	had	
do	did	done		hear	heard	heard	
draw	drew	drawn		hide	hid	hidden	

1. When *hang* means "to suspend by a rope, as in a form of capital punishment," then it is a regular verb. The past forms are *hanged*.

BASE FORM	SIMPLE PAST	PAST PARTICIPLE	MEANING	BASE FORM	SIMPLE PAST	PAST PARTICIPLE	MEANING
hit	hit	hit		shut	shut	shut	
hold	held	held		sing	sang	sung	
hurt	hurt	hurt		sink	sank	sunk	
keep	kept	kept		sit	sat	sat	
know	knew	known		sleep	slept	slept	
lay[2]	laid	laid		slide	slid	slid	
lead	led	led		speak	spoke	spoken	
leave	left	left		speed	sped	sped	
lend	lent	lent		spend	spent	spent	
let	let	let		spin	spun	spun	
lie[3]	lay	lain		split	split	split	
light	lit	lit		spread	spread	spread	
lose	lost	lost		stand	stood	stood	
make	made	made		steal	stole	stolen	
mean	meant	meant		stick	stuck	stuck	
meet	met	met		sting	stung	stung	
mistake	mistook	mistaken		stink	stank	stunk	
pay	paid	paid		strike	struck	struck	
put	put	put		swear	swore	sworn	
prove	proved	proved/ proven		sweep	swept	swept	
quit	quit	quit		swim	swam	swum	
read[4]	read	read		swing	swung	swung	
ride	rode	ridden		take	took	taken	
ring	rang	rung		teach	taught	taught	
rise	rose	risen		tear	tore	torn	
run	ran	run		tell	told	told	
say	said	said		think	thought	thought	
see	saw	seen		throw	threw	thrown	
sell	sold	sold		understand	understood	understood	
send	sent	sent		upset	upset	upset	
set	set	set		wake	woke	woken	
shake	shook	shaken		wear	wore	worn	
shoot	shot	shot		win	won	won	
show	showed	shown		withdraw	withdrew	withdrawn	
shrink	shrank	shrunk		write	wrote	written	

2. *Lay* means "to set or place something on a surface." It is always followed by a noun. Example: I laid my book on the desk.
3. *Lie* means "to rest or lie down, such as on a sofa or bed." When *lie* means "to tell a false statement," it is a regular verb: *lie–lied–lied*.
4. The present form of *read* is pronounced "reed." The simple past and past participle forms are pronounced "red."

INDEX

PHOTO CREDITS

ALAMY
pp. 19, 34: Pictorial Press Ltd.
p. 36: Photos 12. p. 55: Richard
Levine. p. 62 (top): Allstar Picture
Library. p. 102 (bottom): Richard
Levine. p. 125: Presselect. p. 126:
Pictorial Press Ltd.

CP IMAGES
p. 33: Features (1370546s).
p. 96 (bottom): AP Photo/Shizuo
Kambayashi.

GAETZ, LYNNE
pp. 67, 76 (top).

ISTOCKPHOTO
p. 59: ZoneCreative. p. 73:
Willsie. p. 74: Radu Razvan. p. 94:
franckreporter. p. 96 (top):
WEKWEK. p. 105: GYI NSEA.
p. 117 (bottom): Elkor. p. 121
(bottom): Solidago. p. 124:
webphotographeer. p. 130 (top):
Andrew Rich; (bottom): Jen
Grantham. p. 133 (bottom):
Rosemarie Gearhart. pp. 135,
142: MorePixels. p. 137: Nancy
Nehring. p. 142 (bottom): Robert
Guenther. p. 143: Ryan Lane.

PHOTOTHÈQUE ERPI
p. 5 (centre).

SHUTTERSTOCK
pp. 1 (top), 12: Joao Virissimo.
p. 1 (bottom): Mikhail Zahranichny.
p. 4: Paul Prescott. p. 5 (left):
Nip; (right): Olegtoka. p. 6 (top):
Branislav Senic; (bottom): Kzenon.
p. 7: Caitlin Mirra. p. 8 (top, left):
Digital Genetics; (top, right):
A 1Stock; (bottom): GTibbetts.
p. 10: Rafal Sichawa. p. 11:
Tom Wang. p. 13: Gutman/NBC/
NBC NewsWire. pp. 14 (top), 28:

Diego Servo. p. 14 (bottom):
Alspix. p. 17 (shirts): Karina
Balkalyan; (neckties): Terekhov
Igor; (laptop): Alex Starosettsev;
(socks): Olga Popova; (jeans):
Anna Hoychuk; (books): Sergign;
(camera): Skyline; (brush): Lori
Sparikla; (suitcase): Sashkin.
p. 18: Kwest. p. 20: S. Borisov.
p. 21: Oleg Znamenskly. p. 22:
Cherkas. p. 24 (top, left): Tania
Zbrodko; (top, right): Dusica;
(middle, left): Kenneth Sponsler;
(middle, right): Hartphotography;
(bottom, left): Yuri Arcurs; (bottom,
right): Auremar. p. 25 (top, left):
Supri Suhartjoto; (top, centre):
Dudarev Mikhail; (top, right):
Leungchopan; (bottom): Alltoz696.
p. 26: PerseoMedusa. p. 27:
iDesign. p. 28 (left): Andesign101;
(right): Ian Scott. pp. 30 (top), 41:
Refat. p. 35 (top): Maksym
Vlasenko; (bottom): Vertes
Edmond Mihai. p. 37: Sam
Chadwick. p. 38: Joe Seer.
p. 39 (top): Deklofenak; (bottom):
Thorsten Schmitt. pp. 41, 42:
BMCL. p. 43 (top): Supri
Suhartjoto. p. 43 (bottom):
Pertusinas. p. 45: Yuri Arcurs.
p. 46: Sarah Holmlund. p. 47 (top):
Andresr; (bottom): Vectorlib-com.
p. 48: Andrey_l. p. 49: Guido Vrola.
p. 50: Darren Baker. p. 51 (top):
Supri Suhartjoto; (bottom):
Luxorphoto. p. 52: Matej
Pavlansky. p. 53 (top): Alphaspirit.
p. 53: (bottom): Mircea Simu.
p. 56: Subbotina Anna. p. 57:
Marcio Eugenio. p. 58: Gts.
p. 61 (top): Dani3315; (bottom):
Vasily Smirnov. p. 62 (bottom):
Adchariyaphoto. p. 64: Lisa F.
Young. p. 65: mimimilch. p. 66:
svetikd. p. 69: IgorGolovniov.
p. 70 (top): Brian Burton Arsenault;

(bottom, left): Warren Goldswain;
(bottom, centre): Leungchopan;
(bottom, right): Natascha Louwet.
p. 71 (top): Sonya etchison;
(bottom): Scott Prokop. p. 72:
Diego Servo. p. 76: Elnur. p. 77:
Phil Holmes. pp. 78 (top), 87 (top):
M. Pieraccini. p. 78 (bottom): Neo
Edmond. p. 80: Auremar. p. 82:
Karamysh. p. 83: Lo-Random.
p. 84: Magicoven. p. 85: Daniel
Zuckerkandel. p. 86: Aeypix.
p. 87: Tupungato. pp. 89, 101:
MilouSK. p. 92: Apollofoto. p. 93:
Veex. p. 97: Diego Cervo. p. 98:
PressureUA. p. 99: Lisa S. p. 100:
Paul Matthew Photography. p. 102
(top): Dmitry Naumov. pp. 103
(top), 111 (top): Ann Worthy.
p. 103 (bottom): Hfng. p. 106:
Kuzma. p. 107: ARENA Creative.
p. 108: Olly. p. 109: 9nong.
p. 110: Bryan Busovicki. p. 111
(bottom): Marius S. Jurglelewicz.
p. 112: Richard Majlinder. pp. 113
(top), 119 (top): Krivosheev
Vitaly. p. 113 (bottom): Mishella.
p. 115 (top): Iev Radin; (bottom):
Production Studio. p. 116:
Nicholas Moore. p. 117 (top):
Zina Seletskaya. p. 118 (top):
U.Rimages_photo; (bottom):
Romchew. p. 119 (bottom):
Nickpit. p. 120 (top): Olga
Danylenko; (bottom): Regien
Paassen. pp. 121 (top), 133
(top): Radu Razvan. p. 127:
JustASC. p. 128: Stéphane
Bidouze. p. 129: Volodymyr
Goinyk. p. 132: Zoran Karapancev.
p. 133 (middle): Vladimir Koletic.
p. 134: JustASC. p. 138: Geoffrey
Kuchera. p. 139 (top): Muzsy;
(bottom): Alexmillos. p. 141:
Ansar80. p. 144: CROM.